BURT FRANKLIN: RESEARCH & SOURCE WORKS SERIES 417
Selected Essays in History, Economics, & Social Science 110

The Economic and Political Essays of the Ante-Bellum South

The Economic and Political Essays of the Ante-Bellum South

BY

ULRICH B. PHILLIPS

BURT FRANKLIN
NEW YORK

Published by BURT FRANKLIN
235 East 44th St., New York, N.Y. 10017
Originally Published: 1909
Reprinted: 1970
Printed in the U.S.A.

Library of Congress Card Catalog No.: 79-112641
Burt Franklin: Research and Source Works Series 417
Selected Essays in History, Economics, & Social Science 110

ECONOMIC AND POLITICAL ESSAYS IN THE ANTE-BELLUM SOUTH.

N the ante-bellum period and for a generation afterward the Northern people and those of many European countries were profoundly concerned with liberalizing their social and economic institutions and with strengthening their national governments. But in the South the oppressive burden of the great race problem forced the body politic into social conservatism, and at the same time the necessity of insuring exemption from Northern control through Congressional majorities obliged the Southern leaders usually to antagonize nationalistic movements. The great world outside was radical in temper and nationalistic in policy; the South was conservative and stressed the rights of local units under the general government. The world measured the South by its current standards and found the South wanting. The world was not concerned with what the South had to say in its own behalf; it refused to read Southern publications and judged the South unheard. While alien and unfriendly views of the Old South abound to-day in huge editions, the conservative writings of Southerners to the manner born are mostly fugitive and forgotten. Yet on the whole, the Southern product of economic and political essays was very large, and in the mass these writings constitute a varied and often excellent body of literature, highly valuable as interpreting and recording the life and opinions of the successive generations.

As a rule these writings deal not with strictly economic or strictly political themes, but with complex public questions involving economics, politics and society simultaneously. They can be fitted into a plan of treatment only with difficulty and with some danger of slighting significant minor phases in some of the important essays discussed.

Theoretical and General Economics.

Economic theory is, of course, a development of quite recent growth. There was not much discussion of it in America in the ante-bellum period, and few Southerners, in particular, were closet philosophers enough to deal with its refinements. Some of the strongly edited newspapers, such as the *Federal Union* of Milledgeville, Ga., assigned columns regularly to "Political Economy," discussing theoretical questions in them at times, but filling them more generally with concrete items relating to industry and commerce at home and abroad. Among the college professors who wrote on economic themes, Thomas Cooper, long the dominant personality in South Carolina College, schooled a whole generation of budding statesmen in thorough-going *laissez-faire* economic doctrine; Thomas Dew, at William and Mary, and George Tucker, at the University of Virginia, appear to have taught political economy, without special bias, along with various other subjects in social and psychological fields, while J. D. B. DeBow, professor of political economy in the University of Louisiana at New Orleans, probably treated in his lectures more of concrete subjects of American industry and commerce than of unsubstantial theories. Each of these men might well have written general economic treatises, but Tucker and Cooper alone did so.

After a preliminary series of vigorous essays on

banking, public debts, population, etc., written in 1813 and collected into a volume in 1822, Tucker published a scholarly general treatise on money and banking in 1839, and a statistical analysis of the United States census returns in 1843. Cooper's only formal economic writing was his *Lectures on the Elements of Political Economy,* 1826, which embodied the current economic thought of the *laissez-faire* school. He, of course, advocated free trade and free banking. Incidentally, he estimated slave labor, under the existing conditions in the cotton belt, to be more expensive than free labor. Dew apparently published nothing noteworthy except his famous essay on slavery, 1833, while DeBow contented himself with editing his *Review* and a cyclopedic description of Southern and Western resources in 1853-54, superintending the eighth United States census, writing a compendium of that census, 1854, and issuing occasional articles on the plantation system and the project of reopening the foreign slave trade. Aside from the writings of these few professional economic philosophers, the South produced practically nothing in economic theory or in formal statistics. Robert Mills' *Statistics of South Carolina,* 1826, and George White's *Statistics of Georgia,* 1849, were mere historical and descriptive miscellanies.

Agriculture.

Few Southerners were pen-and-ink men by native disposition. Most of them wrote for publication only under the pressure of public emergency. In easy times the reading class of Southerners would read the ancient and modern European classics, and the local newspapers would be concerned mainly with world politics. But in times of industrial crises thinking men would inquire for economic and social treatises throwing light upon American problems;

the newspapers would teem with essays on the causes, character and remedies of the existing depression, and the job-presses would issue occasional books and numerous pamphlets by local authors upon the issues of the day.

In Southern agriculture each occurrence of a crisis brought forth substantial writings, whether soil surveys, descriptions of methods, or didactic essays. Near the end of the Eighteenth century, for example, occurred a severe depression in Carolina coast industry, and in 1802 appeared Drayton's *View of South Carolina,* describing methods and improvements in indigo, rice and cotton, and in 1808 Ramsay's *History of South Carolina* was published, with a large appendix full of agricultural data from and for the sea-island district. During the War of 1812 tobacco was heavily depressed, and John Taylor, of Caroline, began to write his *Arator* essays for newspaper and pamphlet publication.* In the late twenties the Eastern cotton belt felt the pinch of Western competition, and in 1828 was established at Charleston the *Southern Agriculturist,* a strongly edited monthly which was well supported by subscribers and contributors for several years until the return of easy times. From 1839 to 1844 was the most severe economic depression in the history of the ante-bellum South. Cotton was principally affected, but all other interests suffered in sympathy. The result was an abundant activity in economic writing, agriculture included. Edmund Ruffin, who had long been conspicuous as a soil and crop expert in Virginia, was employed by the commonwealth of South Carolina to make an agricultural survey of the state, made his first descriptive report in 1843, and published occasional essays and addresses during the next decade upon soils and fertilizers. R. F. W. Allston, a sea-island planter, published in 1843 a memoir on rice planting (as well as a general descriptive essay in 1854 on Southern seacoast crops), and in 1844 Whitemarsh B. Seabrook, president of the South Carolina Agricultural Society, afterward governor of the state, published a memoir upon the development of sea-island cotton culture.

All of these publications were soon eclipsed in importance by the establishment of the famous and invaluable *DeBow's Review* at New Orleans in 1846, which for many years afterward not only abounded in contributed articles and news items upon agricultural and other economic subjects, but also reprinted most of the noteworthy fugitive addresses and essays which appeared in the field of Southern economics during the period of the *Review's* publication. The *Cotton Planters' Manual*, compiled by J. A. Turner, of Georgia (1857), deserves mention as a collection of useful essays reprinted from various sources on cotton culture, plant diseases, manures and commerce. On the sugar industry, nothing was written in the United States of value comparable to several essays in the West Indies: Clement Caines, *Letters on the Cultivation of the Otaheite Cane* (London, 1801), the anonymous *Practical Rules for the Management and Medical Treatment of Negro Slaves in the Sugar Colonies* (London, 1803), and M. G. Lewis' *Journal of a West India Proprietor* (London, 1834).

Mining, Manufactures, Transportation and Commerce.

Upon the subject of mining, all Southern colonial and ante-bellum literature is negligible after the time of William Byrd's excellent description of the Virginia iron mines about 1732. West Virginia salt, Tennessee copper and Georgia gold were neglected by all but newspaper writers, while Carolina phosphates, Alabama iron, Louisiana sulphur and Texas oil did not begin to be mined until after the ante-bellum period.

On manufactures, William Gregg published a series of articles in the *Charleston Courier* and collected them in a pamphlet, 1845. He described the prior attempts at textile manufacturing in South Carolina, attributing their ill-success to the smallness of the scale of operation and the failure of each mill to specialize in a single sort of cloth; and he urged more extensive embarkation upon manufacturing and the avoidance of past errors. Aside from factory officials in their company reports and occasional descriptive, apologetical and hortatory writers in *DeBow's Review*, Gregg, with his slender writing, seems to have been alone in the field.

In the field of transportation there were innumerable essays and reports upon local problems, projects and progress in the improvement of transit facilities. Among them the treatise of Robert Mills on a project of public works in South Carolina, 1822, is notable for its elaboration and pretentiousness and for the complete impracticability of his plans. Robert Y. Hayne's essays and reports on the Charleston and Cincinnati railroad project, 1837-39, were similarly chimerical, as were also some of the Alabama writings on plank roads about 1850. To offset the recklessness of such writings as these, an anonymous writer published a notable series of ultra-conservative essays in the *Charleston Mercury* and collected them in a pamphlet, *The Railroad Mania, By Anti-Debt*, Charleston, 1848. In the main the Southern essays in the field of transportation were distinctly sane and well reasoned. Some of the official railroad reports are distinctly valuable as noting general economic developments in their territory year by year. Among such are the reports of the Central of Georgia officers, which were collected and reprinted by the company in occasional volumes.

The genius of the Southern people ran very slightly to commerce, and their literature shows little attention to any but a few of its spectacular features. The principal themes attracting the newspaper and periodical writers (and there were practically no others dealing with commerce) were the importance of cotton in the world's commerce, the possibility of cornering the cotton supply or otherwise manipulating its price in the interest of the producers, the project of establishing direct trade in steamship lines between Southern ports and Europe, and thereby attempting to reduce the Northern profits on Southern commerce, and the possibility of reopening the African slave trade. The cotton trade discussions were most conspicuous about 1836 to 1839, the study of foreign commercial relations was mainly in the fifties, and the debate over the slave trade was waged, between a few advocates and numerous opponents, between 1855 and 1861.

Labor.

White wage-earning labor was probably not so extremely scarce in the ante-bellum South as most historians would have us believe, but trades-unions were few, and the labor problems apart from negroes and slavery were not conspicuous enough to occasion the writing of many formal essays. Joseph Henry Lumpkin, later chief justice of Georgia, published, in 1852, an essay, *The Industrial Regeneration of the South,* which gives his interpretation of existing conditions, incidentally, in his somewhat

utopian argument in favor of manufactures. He
says, in part:

"It is objected that these manufacturing establishments will become
the hotbeds of crime * * *   But I am by no means ready to concede
that our poor, degraded, half-fed, half-clothed and ignorant population,
without Sabbath schools, or any other kind of instruction, mental or
moral, or without any just appreciation of character,—will be injured
by giving them employment, which will bring them under the oversight
of employers who will inspire them with self-respect by taking an interest in their welfare."

The pros and cons of employing free labor for
plantation work were discussed in newspaper articles, but probably the best journalistic item in this
connection is that of the traveler-scientist, Charles
Lyell, written in 1846 and published in his *Second
Visit to the United States* (Vol. II., p. 127):

"The sugar and cotton crop is easily lost if it is not taken in at once
when it is ripe * * *   Very lately a planter, five miles below New
Orleans, having resolved to dispense with slave labor, hired one hundred
Irish and German emigrants at very high wages. In the middle of the
harvest they all struck for double pay. No others were to be had, and
it was impossible to purchase slaves in a few days. In that time he lost
produce to the value of ten thousand dollars."

Negroes.

The Southerners of the plantation districts were
as familiar with the typical plantation negroes as
they were with typical cows and horses. Thomas
Jefferson, in his *Notes on Virginia* (Query 14),
characterized negroes as improvident, sensuous, in-
constant, well endowed in memory, poor in reason-
ing power and dull in imagination. Few, aside from
Jefferson, thought it necessary to describe the obvious. In the West Indies, where for many decades
the volume of slave imports was enormous and
where the fresh Africans were representative of all
the diverse tribes from Senegal and Abyssinia to
Good Hope and Madagascar, the planters were
prompted to compare the tribal traits and thus to

publish discussions of negro characteristics in general. But in the continental South, in the antebellum period, the tribal stocks, Berber, Coromantee, Ebo, Congo, Kaffir, Hottentot, etc., had become blended into the relatively constant type of the American plantation negro. As a familiar item in the white man's environment, the negro was not to be described or interpreted, but was rather to be accepted and adjusted. Dr. J. C. Nott, of Mobile, at the middle of the Nineteenth century, like Mr. F. L. Hoffman at the end of it, was led to study and publish upon negro traits by reason of his interest in life insurance. Dr. S. A. Cartwright, of New Orleans, in the same period as Nott, was led into a general study of the negro by his interest in negro diseases. Practically all the other writers approached the subject of the negro as a corollary to the question of the perpetuity of slavery. Dr. J. H. Van Evrie, of Washington, later of New York, voiced the dominant opinion when he wrote (1853) that the ills of the South were mainly attributable not to slavery, but to the negro. In 1861 Van Evrie further elaborated his unflattering opinion of the negro in his book, *Negroes and Slavery,* which he reprinted in 1867 with the title, *White Supremacy and Negro Subordination.* Van Evrie, as usual with controversialists, falls into the error of proving too much.

In the case of anti-slavery writers, whether Northern or Southern, it required the abolition of slavery to reveal the negro as a concrete phenomenon. H. R. Helper was the most extreme example of this. His *Impending Crisis* (1857) denounced the institution of slavery with the greatest vigor as the cause of all the Southern ills, but his *Nojoque* (1867) was devoted to a still more absurdly extreme denunciation of the negro as a worthless encumbrance and a curse.   It is curious that extremely little was published upon the mulatto element, except a few essays upon the orthodox but indefensible theme that by reason of their shortness of life, their infertility and their moral degeneracy, the mixed breed formed a negligible though vicious fraction of the population.

Slavery.

The economic and social aspects of slavery furnished a bulk of essays only equalled in the South by that upon the political bearings of the same institution of domestic servitude.   In the colonial period the discussion was abundant, sane, and matter-of-fact, so far as may be judged from indirect evidence, but little of it went into print.   In the period of the Revolution the discussion was so hysterical in tone that it resulted at the South more in reaction than in liberalism.

The great ante-bellum debate on the subject brought forth an extreme variety of essays, both as to scope and tone, but the general inclination of the writers, with the notable exception of Helper, was to confront conditions, not theories.   Before 1833 the discussion in the South tended to be a humdrum rehashing of time-honored views, relieved by an occasional reflection of the ideas of the European economists.   James Raymond wrote an essay on the *Comparative Cost of Free and Slave Labor in Agriculture* in 1827, which was awarded a prize by the Frederick County, Maryland, Agricultural Society.   His argument follows the line of Adam Hodgson's reply to J. B. Say's discarded early views: the farmer needs an elastic supply of labor, and hireling labor is suited for this while slave labor is not; slaves are lazy, slipshod, wasteful, as contrasted with the carefulness, efficiency and frugality of freemen.   Raymond, of course, like the typical abolitionist, divorced the slavery issue from the negro issue by ignoring the question of what would become of the great mass of Southern negroes when freed. Raymond also ignored the fact that in the principal Southern industries, under the plantation system, regularity was more to be desired than elasticity in the labor supply, and that slavery secured the desired constancy in the number of laborers available. The publication of Professor Dew's famous essay in 1833, prompted by the debate upon projects for abolition in the Virginia legislature in 1831-32, demonstrated that the slavery question was essentially a phase of the great negro question. After censuring the recklessness of the Virginia debate, and showing that slavery had been a highly serviceable institution in furthering human progress in many countries and in many centuries, Dew analyzes the American situation and the proposals for its betterment. He condemns the several plans, varying in detail, for the emancipation and deportation of the negroes on the grounds of the excessive cost of the process, the threatened paralysis of plantation industry, and the inability of the negroes to maintain their own welfare if deported to Africa. He condemns still more strongly all plans for abolition which do not include provision for deportation, pointing out the social and industrial dangers of freeing an irresponsible population, and pointing to the record of the Northern free negroes and to the chaotic state of affairs in Hayti as warnings. After Dew's essay no writer could secure countenance in the South for any anti-slavery plans unless he could show some means of readjusting the negro population in a way not endangering the security of the whites or threatening the general welfare.

In close harmony with Dew's argument, essays were written in the thirties and forties by Chancel-

lor William Harper and Gov. J. H. Hammond, both
of South Carolina, which were reprinted in 1852
along with Dew's essay and a slender one by W. G.
Simms, in a volume entitled the *Pro-Slavery Argument*. Harper, following Dew's theme in general,
lays main stress upon the civilizing and tranquiliz-
ing effects of slavery. Hammond's essay, written
in the form of a reply to Thomas Clarkson's attacks
upon slavery, is an exceptionally strong apology for
the institution. He concedes that slave labor is expensive, by reason of the slave's first cost and the
expense of feeding, clothing and sheltering him and
his family in infancy, sickness and old age, in bad
seasons as well as good; and he prophesies that any
great increase in the density of population will
cause the abandonment of slavery by making free
labor available and cheaper. Meanwhile, in view
of the sparseness of the Southern population and
the unfitness of the negroes for the stress of competition, he deprecates any radical readjustments
and resents extraneous interference.

Numerous other Southern essayists clamored for
public attention, of whom only the more significant
can here be noted. John Fletcher, of Louisiana, in
1851 issued a bulky primer to prove the goodness of
slavery, in easy lessons and with main reference to
Holy Writ. George S. Sawyer, also of Louisiana,
gave an elaborate eulogy of slavery upon historical
and ethical grounds in his *Southern Institutes*
(1859). Henry Hughes, in pamphlets of 1858-59,
tried to bolster up slavery by the euphemistic device
of changing its name to warranteeism, and thereby
indicating that its purpose was to maintain industrial
order rather than to exploit the laboring class; but
Hughes could not get an audience even in the South
for his ineffective plea. Daniel Christy, of Cincinnati, entitling his book *Cotton is King* (1855), mag-

nified the economic efficiency and vital importance of slavery as a divinely established institution. Though Christy may not have been a Southerner, his book was adopted by the Southern ultramontanists as their own. Professor A. T. Bledsoe, of the University of Virginia, in his book *An Essay on Liberty and Slavery* (1856), endeavored to refute seventeen specific fallacies of the abolitionists, and to vindicate slavery and all its works, including the fugitive slave law. In 1860 E. N. Elliott, "President of Planters' College, Mississippi," bought the authors' rights to Christy's and Bledsoe's books, secured new scriptural arguments for slavery from Dr. Stringfellow, of Virginia, and Dr. Hoge, of New Jersey, and an ethnological essay from Dr. Cartwright, of New Orleans, added to these Hammond's and Harper's already standard essays, and the text of the Dred-Scott decision by the United States Supreme Court, printed the whole in one bulky subscription volume, *Cotton is King and Pro-Slavery Arguments* (1860), and sold it in great numbers to the planters and townsmen on the eve of the war. The book, on the whole, compares very unfavorably with the more modest but substantial *Pro-Slavery Argument* of 1852.

More notable as a contribution to thought are the two books by George Fitzhugh, of Virginia, with the curious titles: *Sociology for the South, or the Failure of Free Society* (1854), and *Cannibals All, or Slaves Without Masters* (1857). Declaring himself an outright socialist, Fitzhugh denounces the whole modern system of wage-labor, and contends that laborers on hire are subject to more severe exploitation than laborers in bondage. He advocates benevolent despotism on general principles, and particularly where applied to a class so little capable of self-protection as the negroes in America. He holds up

the Southern plantation system for the admiration
of all socialists, communists, or other paternalists.
Fitzhugh, however, injures the effect of his books
by his own loquacity. He adds chapters at random
championing the South against the North in every
possible connection, and thereby lets it seem;
whether justly or not, that he is a socialist only for
the sake of the argument.

As an assault upon the general position held by
the whole group of writers above treated, Hinton R.
Helper, of North Carolina, issued his startling book,
The Impending Crisis of the South (1857). He
points out the relative economic stagnation in the
South, asserts that slavery is its sole cause, and denounces the slave-holding class as a cruel and wicked
oligarchy conspiring for the oppression of the negroes and non-slave-holding whites alike. Helper
is a past master in the art of leaping at conclusions
and concealing the feat by outbursts of perfervid
rhetoric. Helper was the spokesman of a group of
radical Southern non-slaveholders, but he secured
relatively little Southern endorsement on the whole
because he failed to meet adequately the vital problem of what to do with the negro population in the
event of the abolition of slavery. But the North
bought fifty thousand copies in three years, and at
the North, where Helper's *Nojoque* has always been
unknown, his *Impending Crisis* is still considered by
thousands to be the soundest of interpretations.

Daniel R. Goodloe, of North Carolina, was a much
more substantial though less glittering opponent of
slavery. In his pamphlet of 1846, *Inquiry Into the
Causes Which Have Retarded the Accumulation of
Wealth and Increase of Population in the Southern
States,* he presented most of the data which Helper
used ten years later, along with some interpretations which were too deep for Helper to grasp. To

the time-honored criticism that slavery hampered industrial progress by stigmatizing labor, Goodloe added a thought which he had worked out that a still more important phase of the burdensome character of slavery lay in its devoting a huge volume of capital to the purchase and control of laborers. He showed that by buying laborers instead of hiring them the South had long been sinking money and depriving itself of resources which might have been used to great advantage in the development of large-scale manufacturing and commerce.

The final ante-bellum word upon the burdensomeness of slavery and its actual and prospective decadence was written by George M. Weston, who seems to have come from Maine and lived mostly in Washington, and at Washington to have gotten into sympathetic touch with the clearest thinkers on slavery, and also to have read well a wide variety of pertinent literature. In his book, *The Progress of Slavery in the United States* (1857), he shows the relatively stagnant condition of the slave-holding communities, discussing the reasons therefor, he points out the encroaching of the free-labor system within the border of the slave-holding section, prophesying a still further restriction by economic process of the area and importance of slave-holding industry, he demonstrates that the then current agitation for the congressional increase of slave-holding territory was purely political in character and offered no economic advantage to the captains of industry in the active plantation districts, and he foretells that the decadence and disappearance of slavery will inure to the benefit instead of the injury of the South. To the careful student of Southern history it may well appear that Weston's little-known book was more representative of the views of well-informed and thoughtful Southerners than

were the manifestoes of the politicians. In those years of excited controversy just preceding the war, public opinion in the South, of course, opposed any revision of opinions in the face of the enemy. Public expressions of doubts as to the perfect efficiency and goodness of the slavery system were discouraged at the time. But there is little doubt that many substantial Southerners held many of the views which Hammond, Goodloe and Weston expressed. Among the evidences of this may be cited the essays of representative keen Southern students, of the following generation, who it is most reasonable to suppose expressed much of what had existed, even though the ideas may have been latent, in the minds of thoughtful men in the ante-bellum years. Among the essays in point may be mentioned: W. L. Trenholm, *The Southern States, Their Social and Industrial History, Conditions and Needs,* published in the Transactions of the American Social Science Association for September, 1877, and J. C. Reed, *The Old and New South* (1876), reprinted in the Appendix to the same author's *The Brother's War* (1905).

Social Surveys.

As a general treatise upon social types, D. R. Hundley's *Social Relations in Our Southern States* (1860) stands alone among the productions of Southern writers. Born in the South, the author says his education "was chiefly acquired at Southern institutions of learning, in the states of Alabama, Tennessee, Kentucky and Virginia," and was completed by a course in law at Harvard. His collegiate migrations would indicate a waywardness of disposition somewhat characteristic of well-to-do Southern youth in the period, and his waywardness crops out at many places where flippant digressions and gibes at the North mar the character of his book. Nevertheless, Hundley was widely traveled, closely observant, keen in analysis and facile in characterization, and his book is valuable accordingly. His chapters on the Southern gentleman, the Southern middle class, the Southern yeoman, the poor-white and the cotton snob, as he calls the *nouveau riche* of the South, are particularly useful contributions. He gives good fragmentary data, also, upon student dissipation, upon slave traders and upon negro conditions generally, including a notice of the social distinctions which prevailed among the slaves.

William Gilmore Simms, in his *Southward Ho* (1854), gives informal sketches of society in Virginia and the Carolinas, from the point of view of one who was at the same time a middle-class South Carolinian and a citizen of the world. Joseph Baldwin's *Flush Times of Alabama* (1853), a semi-humorous work, is the chief writing upon society in the Southwest.

Political Essays; Theoretical.

Southern writings upon the abstract theory of government were as scarce as we have seen those to have been in theoretical economics. Practically all state papers are negligible as essays in political theory, including Jefferson's Declaration of Independence and Mason's Virginia Bill of Rights, for each of these was merely a brilliantly phrased set of ideas borrowed from current European philosophy, and applied concretely to interpret and justify the American problems and policy of the moment. The writings of Francis Lieber, notable as they are, ought hardly to be claimed as of Southern production, for although Lieber was a professor in South Carolina College for many years and wrote all of his principal books there, he never ceased to be an

alien in the Southern country. With his mind always dominated by German idealistic devotion to
liberty and revolution, he could feel nothing but
repugnance at the conditions in the midst of which
he sojourned and at the philosophy of the people
who, against his preference, were his neighbors.
Lieber's books would indicate that he never con-
fronted any of the distinctive Southern problems of
concrete racial adjustments. There remain for mention here only St. George Tucker and John C. Calhoun, each of whom had the United States constitution conspicuously in mind when writing upon
government in general, and each of whom was a full-
fledged product and a spokesman of the Southern
community. Tucker's essay, published as an appendix to his edition of Blackstone's *Commentaries*
(1803), championed the Eighteenth century doctrine of inherent rights and the social compact, and
applied it elaborately in interpreting the Federal
system of the United States. By correlating the
position of the states in the Federal compact with
the position of individuals in the theoretical social
compact, he, of course, provided a basis for reason-
ing out the supremacy of the states and the subordi-
nate character of the central government. He
proceeded to state expressly as an inevitable deduc-
tion from his general scheme of political philosophy,
that the several states had an indefeasible right of
seceding from any Federation or Union which they
had entered or might enter.

Calhoun organized his formal writing in political
philosophy into two treatises written shortly before
his death. Of these, the *Disquisition on Government* (1851), as Professor W. A. Dunning has well
said, "is in some respects the most original and
the most profound political essay in American literature. It is by no means a complete philosophy of

the state, nor is its relation to the concrete issues of the day much disguised; but it penetrates to the very roots of all political and social activity, and presents, if it does not satisfactorily solve, the ultimate intellectual problems in this phase of human existence." In bald outline the thread of the essay is as follows: Society is necessary to man, and government is necessary to society; but governments tend to infringe upon the just liberties and rights of individuals, and popular governments are no less prone toward this oppression than are monarchies, for the reason that popular majorities are prone to consider their own interests as the only ones which the government ought to promote, and prone accordingly to ignore and override the interests and rights of minorities. The suffrage franchise alone will not safeguard the individual against oppression. Just as governments are instituted to secure the weak against the strong, constitutions are established in large part to restrain the governments when controlled by strong interests from overriding minority rights. To limit the government properly in this regard without unduly weakening it is a most delicate and difficult problem, and one which the framers of the American Federal constitution did not fully solve. This is the profound problem as seen by Calhoun. His prescription of a remedy is less strong than his diagnosis of the trouble. He proposes a system of concurrent majorities by which each great interest in the country should be put into control of one branch of the legislative power of the government, and thereby be given a veto power upon measures proposed by each other great interest. Calhoun's plan is not fully adequate for the solution of the problem, but neither is any other plan ever yet devised by any philosopher or any nation.

Constitutional Construction.

Whenever in Federal politics of the ante-bellum period a majority in Congress overrode the opposition, or was about to override it, upon an important issue, it was a fairly constant practice for the spokesman of the minority to appeal to the constitution and declare the programme of the majority to be an exercise by the Government of unwarranted powers. The majority, of course, could often ride rough-shod and had little need of resorting to pamphlets and treatises to defend its constitutional position. Quires were written in championship of broad construction, but reams for strict construction; and it happened that most of strict construction writers were men of the South. Madison's articles in the *Federalist* may be dismissed as being devoted to explanation and eulogy rather than to the construction of the constitution. Madison soon reacted from his nationalistic position and wrote the Virginia Resolutions (1798), which, with Jefferson's Kentucky Resolutions, adopted in minority remonstrance against the Alien and Sedition acts of Congress, served for many years as the official embodiment of constitutional construction for the state-rights school. Shortly afterward, in 1803, John Marshall began his series of vigorous nationalistic decisions which averaged more than one per year for the next thirty years, accompanying the decisions of his court in most of these cases with fulminations from his own pen to preach the doctrines of broad construction. Henry Clay, who, aside from Webster, was the principal other spokesman in the United States for broad construction, contributed no arguments of note upon constitutional topics, but confined himself largely to arguments on the grounds of expediency, making special use of the *argumentum ad hominem.* The several steps taken by Marshall and Clay gave the chief occasions for the publication of strict construction arguments by the opposing school. The principal essayists who were spurred immediately by Marshall were the Virginians, Spencer Roane and John Taylor, of Caroline. Roane, who as chief justice of Virginia had the chagrin of seeing some of his own state-rights decisions reversed by Marshall's court on appeal, resorted to the public press in remonstrance. His principal series of articles was printed in the *Richmond Inquirer* in May-August, 1821, and collected in a pamphlet entitled *The Letters of Algernon Sidney*. Taylor issued a succession of polemical books: *Inquiry Into the Principles and Policy of the Government of the United States* (1813), expressing his disrelish of the consolidation tendencies of the time; *Construction Construed* (1820), denouncing the McCulloch *vs*. Maryland decision and asserting the sovereignty of the states; *Tyranny Unmasked* (1822), denying the power of the Federal Supreme Court to assign limits to the spheres of state and Federal authority, and advocating a state veto for emergency use in curbing Federal encroachment, and *New Views of the Constitution* (1823), which reiterated his former contention and stressed the value of the states as champions of sectional interests against injury by hostile congressional majorities.

Clay's campaign for his "American System" drew fire mainly from the South Carolinians. In 1827 Robert J. Turnbull, under the pseudonym of Brutus, published a series of thirty-three articles in the *Charleston Mercury,* and promptly issued them in a pamphlet entitled *The Crisis: Or Essays on the Usurpation of the Federal Government,* which he dedicated "to the people of the 'Plantation States' as a testimony of respect, for their rights

of sovereignty.'' Turnbull vehemently urged the
people of the South to face the facts, to realize that
the North was beginning to use its control of Congress for Southern oppression by protective tariffs
and otherwise; and he proposed as a remedy that
South Carolina should promptly interpose her own
sovereignty and safeguard Southern interests by
vetoing such congressional acts as she should decide
to be based upon Federal usurpations and intended
for Northern advantage at the cost of Southern oppression.   McDuffie and Hayne promptly assumed
the leadership of the state-sovereignty-and-South-
ern-rights cause in Congress and many other promi-
nent South Carolinians fell in line, including the
editors R. B. Rhett and J. H. Hammond, and including most conspicuously John C. Calhoun, who
drafted nearly all the state papers of South Carolina during the nullification episode, and who, in
addition, issued powerful memorials upon the issues
of the day over his own signature.   These writings
are too prominently a part of American history to
require any detailed discussion here.

The final issue prompting state sovereignty expressions was that of negro slavery.   The principal
work in this group was Calhoun's *Discourse on the
Constitution and Government of the United States*
(1851), which supplements his *Disquisition on Government,* already outlined.   This *Discourse* follows
the theme of his more general *Disquisition,* applying
its contentions more specifically to the American
Federal problem; it champions concurrent majorities again, champions the historical doctrine of
state sovereignty and defends, in somewhat subdued
phrase, his former pet plan of nullification.   The
Discourse and the *Disquisition* were Calhoun's political testament; the great obituary of the state
sovereignty and secession movement was Alexander

H. Stephens' *Constitutional View of the War between the States,* which, as a post-bellum work, falls beyond our present scope.

Party Politics.

It was the custom of but a few leaders to address their constituents for party purposes through essays instead of from the hustings. One of these was Robert Goodloe Harper, who, upon his retirement from Congress in 1801, addressed to his South Carolina constituents a eulogistic but sane and vigorous memoir upon the constructive work of his party: *A Letter Containing a Short View of the Political Principles of the Federalists, and of the Situation in Which They Found and Left the Government.* Another was Edward Livingston, who, when asking for reëlection to Congress in 1825, issued an *Address to the Electors of the Second District of Louisiana,* which is notable for his attempt to reconcile. the desire of the sugar planters for protection to their own industry with the disrelish of the cotton planters for the policy of protection in general, by the device of calling the duty on sugar a revenue item and not a protective item in the tariff schedules. Various other candidates, of course, issued electioneering pamphlets, practically all of which are negligible as essays. On a plan combining an historical sketch with political propaganda were several writings such as Thomas Cooper's *Consolidation: An Account of Parties in the United States, from the Convention of 1787 to the Present Period* (1824), written, of course, with a state-rights purpose; Henry A. Wise's *Seven Decades of the Union,* eulogizing John Tyler and the policy of the state-rights Whigs, and such biographies as J. F. H. Claiborne's *Life and Correspondence of John A. Quitman* (1860), which contains secession propaganda on the au-

thor's own account along with the biography of
Quitman.

Sectionalism.

Instead of making a catalogue of the many essays
which deal with petty sectionalism within the several states and with grand sectionalism between the
North and the South, we will conclude our view of
economic and political writings by presenting the
theme of William H. Trescott's *The Position and
Course of the South* (1850), as an embodiment of
the soundest realization of the sectional conditions
and prospects of the Southern section in the closing
decade of the ante-bellum period. The author, a
leading, experienced, conservative citizen of South
Carolina, states in his preface, dated Oct. 12, 1850,
that his purpose is to unify the widely separated
parts of the South. He says his views are not new,
but they are characteristically Southern: ''We are
beginning to think for ourselves, the first step toward acting for ourselves.'' The essay begins with
an analysis of industrial contrasts. He says that
in the slavery system the relation of capital and
labor is moral—labor is a duty, in the wage-earning
system the relation is legal—the execution of contract. The contract system, he says, promotes constant jealousy and friction between capital and
labor, while the slavery system secures peace by
subordinating labor to capital. The political majority of the North represents labor; that of the
South, capital; the contrast is violent. Free labor
hates slave labor, and will overturn the system if it
can. The two sections with many contrasting and
conflicting characteristics are combined under the
United States constitution, but they are essentially
irreconcilable. Even in foreign relations the North
is jealous of foreign powers for commercial and
industrial reasons, while Southern industry is not

competitive with, but complementary to European industry and commerce, and the South, if a nation by itself, would be upon most cordial terms with foreign powers. "The United States government under the control of Northern majorities must reflect Northern sentiment, sustain Northern interests, impersonate Northern power. Even if it be conceded that the South has no present grievance to complain of, it is the part of wisdom to consider the strength and relations of the sections, and face the question, what is the position of the South? In case our rights should be attacked, where is our constitutional protection? The answer is obvious. If the expression of outraged feeling throughout our Southern land be anything but the wild ravings of wicked faction, it is time for the South to act firmly, promptly and forever. But one course is open to her honor, and that is secession and the formation of an independent confederacy. There are many men grown old in the Union who would feel an honest and pardonable regret at the thought of its dissolution. They have prided themselves on the success of the great American experiment of political self-government, and feel that the dissolution of the Union would proclaim a mortifying failure. Not so. The vital principle of political liberty is representative government, and when Federal arrangements are discarded, that lives in original vigor. Who does not consider the greatest triumph of the British constitution the facility and vigor with which, under slight modifications, it developed into the great republican government under which we have accomplished our national progress. And so it will be with the United States constitution. The experiment of our fathers will receive its highest illustration, and a continent of great republics, equal, independent and allied, will demonstrate to the world the capabilities of republican constitutional government. We believe that Southern interests demand an independent government. We believe that the time has now come when this can be established temperately, wisely, strongly. But in effecting this separation we would not disown our indebtedness, our gratitude to the past. The Union has spread Christianity, fertilized a wilderness, enriched the world's commerce wonderfully, spread Anglo-Saxon civilization. "It has given to the world sublime names, which the world will not willingly let die—heroic actions which will light the eyes of a far-coming enthusiasm. It has achieved its destiny. Let us achieve ours."

BIBLIOGRAPHY.—Acton, Lord: *The Civil War in America* (1866, reprinted as Chap. IV. of his *Historical Essays and Studies*, London, 1907); Allston, R. F. W.: *Memoir of the Introduction and Planting of Rice in South Carolina* (Charleston, 1843), and *Sea-Coast Crops of the South* (1854, reprinted in *DeBow's Review*, XVI., 589–615); Baldwin, Jos. G.: *The Flush Times of Alabama and Mississippi, A Series of Sketches* (New York, 1853); Calhoun, J. C.: *Works* (Charleston, 1851, New York, 1853–5); Cooper, Thos.: *Consolidation: An Account of Parties in the United States, from the Convention of 1787 to the Present Period* (published anonymously, Columbia, 1824), and *Lectures on the Elements of Political Economy* (Columbia, 1826); DeBow, J. D. B.: *The Industrial Resources, etc., of the Southern and Western States* (New Orleans, 1853–4); Dunning, W. A.: *American Political Philosophy* (in the *Yale Reveiw*, August, 1895); Elliott, E. N.: *Cotton Is King and Pro-Slavery Arguments Comprising the Writings of Hammond, Harper, Christy, Stringfellow, Hodge, Bledsoe, and Cartwright on This Important Subject* (Augusta, 1860); Fitzhugh, Geo.: *Cannibals All, or Slaves Without Masters* (Richmond, 1857), and *Sociology for the South, or The Failure of Free Society* (Richmond, 1854); Fletcher, John: *Studies on Slavery in Easy Lessons* (Natchez, 1852); Goodloe, D. R.: *Inquiry into the Causes which have Retarded the Accumulation of Wealth and Increase of Population in the Southern States* (Washington, 1846). (This essay is said by S. B. Weeks to have been written in 1841; it was published first in the *New York American*, 1844, and in several places thereafter); Gregg, Wm.: *Essays on Domestic Industry, or an Inquiry into the Expediency of Establishing Cotton Manufactures in South Carolina* (Charleston, 1845); Harper, Robert Goodloe: *Select Works* (Baltimore, 1814); [Harrison, Jesse Burton]: *Review of the Slave Question, Extracted from the American Quarterly Review, December, 1832, Showing That Slavery is a Hindrance to Prosperity, by a Virginian* (Richmond, 1833); Helper, H. R.: *The Impending Crisis of the South: How to*

Meet It (New York, 1857), and *Nojoque, A Question for a Continent* (New York, 1867); Houston, D. F.: *A Critical Study of Nullification in South Carolina* (New York, 1896); Hughes, Henry: *State Liberties: The Right to African Contract Labor* (Port Gibson, Miss., 1858); Hundley, D. R.: *Social Relations in Our Southern States* (New York, 1860); Ingle, Edward, *Southern Sidelights* (New York, 1896); Merriam, C. E.: *The Political Theory of Calhoun* (in the *American Journal of Sociology*, VII., 577–594); Nott, Josiah, C.: *Two Lectures on the Natural History of the Caucasian and Negro Races* (Mobile, 1844); Phillips, U. B.: *The Slave Labor Problem in the Charleston District* (in the *Political Science Quarterly*, XXII., 416–439); *The Pro-Slavery Argument, as maintained by the Most Distinguished Writers of the Southern States, Containing the Several Essays on the Subject, of Chancellor Harper, Governor Hammond, Dr. Simms and Professor Dew* (Charleston, 1852); Ruffin, Edmund: *An Address on the Opposite Results of Exhausting and Fertilizing Systems of Agriculture* (Charleston, 1853), *Calcareous Manures* (2d ed., 1835) and *Report of the Commencement and Progress of the Agricultural Survey of South Carolina for* 1843 (Columbia, 1843); Sawyer, Geo. S.: *Southern Institutes* (Philadelphia, 1858); Seabrook, Whitemarsh B.: *A Memoir on the Origin, Cultivation and Uses of Cotton* (Charleston, 1844); Simms, W. G.: *Southward Ho! A Spell of Sunshine* (New York, 1854); Taylor, John, of Caroline: *Arator, Being a Series of Agricultural Essays, Practical and Political*, by a citizen of Virginia (anonymously published) (Georgetown, D. C., 1813), *Construction Construed* (1822), *Inquiry Into the Principles and Policy of the Government of the United States* (Fredericksburg, 1814), *New Views of the Constitution* (1823) and *Tyranny Unmasked* (Washington, 1822); Trescott, W. H.: *The Position and Course of the South* (Charleston, 1850); Tucker, George: *Essays on Various Subjects of Taste, Morals and National Policy*, by a citizen of Virginia (published anonymously) (Georgetown, D. C., 1822), and *The Theory of Money and Banks Investigated* (Boston, 1839); Tucker, St. George: *Dissertation on Slavery, With a Proposal for Its Gradual Abolition in Virginia* (Philadelphia, 1796, reprinted New York, 1861); Weeks, Stephen B.: *Anti-Slavery Sentiment in the South* (in the *Southern History Association Publications*, II., 87–130); Weston, George M.: *The Progress of Slavery in the United States* (Washington, 1857).

ULRICH B. PHILLIPS

STREET

STREET

A PLAY BY

Joan Aiken

Illustrated by Arvis Stewart

Music by John Sebastian Brown

THE VIKING PRESS
NEW YORK

For my son John,
who wrote the music for this
and my other two plays

First Edition
Text Copyright © Joan Aiken Enterprises, Ltd., 1978
Music Copyright © John Sebastian Brown, 1978
Illustrations Copyright © Viking Penguin, Inc., 1978
All rights reserved · First published in 1978 by The Viking Press
625 Madison Avenue, New York, N.Y. 10022
Published simultaneously in Canada by
Penguin Books Canada Limited
Printed in U.S.A.
1 2 3 4 5 82 81 80 79 78

Library of Congress Cataloging in Publication Data
Aiken, Joan, Street: a play
Summary: A two-act farce about a pair of young lovers
who live in an English village on opposite sides of a
heavily trafficked superhighway.
[1. Plays] I. Stewart, Arvis L. II. Brown, John
Sebastian. III. Title.
PN6120.A5A337   822'.9'14   77-21736
ISBN 0-670-67823-6

PREFACE

Since it is assumed that most productions of this play will be put on in schools or by small theatre groups or by children themselves, the stage directions have been, as far as possible, framed to suit the circumstances of companies with fairly limited resources.

For this reason, many of the directions are more in the nature of suggestions than firm instructions and leave room for improvisation at the discretion of the director. If resources are very limited, the street in *Street* could, for instance, be merely two rows of chairs, facing back to back, with painted paper or cloth representations of houses draped over them; the balconies could be indicated by boxes, folding stepladders, or chairs reversed so that players could stand on the seats. The hamburger stall could be a packing case with imaginary food. Helicopter delivery could be done by a rope over a pulley.

Likewise, the interiors could be indicated simply by a few pieces of furniture—chairs, tables, free-standing bookshelves—from which objects can fall in the Mirkin and Thatcher kitchens—and boxes and barrels in the Spotted Pig.

If it is found impossible for Toomey to saw a hole as required in Act Two, Scene Three, this could be mimed either in view of the audience or partly behind a masking piece of furniture so that Toomey can then crawl offstage out of sight.

The absolutely essential prop is a tape recorder with loud and terrifying sounds of traffic, of the helicopter, and of bulls bellowing and the drumming of hoofs, and soothing bird song for the forest and final scene.

CHARACTERS

MEG MIRKIN	Village witch of Street
HANNIBAL MIRKIN	her sons
TOOMEY MIRKIN	
FRED STEELE	Landlord of the Spotted Pig
LILY STEELE	his daughters
HANNAH STEELE	
SUE THATCHER	Meg's sister-in-law
JENNY THATCHER	Sue's daughter
BERT	a hamburger stallholder
A TRUCK DRIVER	
VILLAGERS	
SEVEN WHITE BULLS	

ACT ONE

ACT TWO

STREET

Act One

SCENE ONE

Empty stage, except for a couple of lampposts near front. Plain backdrop. As many VILLAGERS *as possible, wearing matadors' hats, jeans, carrying short black capes, are grouped expectantly, looking to side of stage.*

VILLAGERS [*joyfully shouting*]: The bulls! The bulls! The bulls are coming!

[*They all dance, leap, and posture exuberantly, then turn and run, with all kinds of elaborate bounds and antics, showing off, and teasing the invisible* BULLS. *A sound of* BULLS *bellowing and the drumming of hoofs grows to high intensity.* HANNIBAL MIRKIN, *scared, climbs up a lamppost.*]

3

VILLAGERS [*mockingly*]: Funky Hannibal Mirkin—
look where Hannibal's lurking!

[*They chant and thumb their noses at him as they run by,
winding in serpentine course over the stage. All go out,
leaving* HANNIBAL *up on his post. The sound of hoofs and
bellowing grows even louder. Shadows of huge* BULLS *pass
across the backdrop. When they are gone, the noise dies
away.* HANNIBAL *descends from the lamppost, picks up
from front of stage an enormous golden key, about as tall
as himself, wraps his black cape over his face, and with
elaborate caution sneaks across stage and out.*

Sound of traffic grows to intensity equal to that of the
BULLS: *brakes squealing, horns hooting, police-car sirens
wailing, etc.*

VILLAGERS *return, slowly, with no exuberance. Several
now have crutches, plaster casts, or slings. They wear
luminous roadworkers' jackets and carry surgical masks
of the same colour. They wheel in the houses, which are
arranged diagonally, three on each side, to suggest village
street. They are reversible flat frames on castors. Exterior
is painted on one side, with various coloured doors, interior on the other, with suggestions of kitchen dressers,
fireplaces, bookshelves, pictures on walls. One house has
an inn sign, The Spotted Pig, over door. Another has two
crossed broomsticks and painted scroll: Village Witch.
These two are opposite each other, farthest away from
stage front. Beyond each is a balcony, which could be a
stepladder. A few road signs could be disposed in corners
of stage: Road Narrows, Double Bend, Bumpy Surface,
School, etc. The two houses nearest the audience have
street signs painted on them: Forest Row on the Spotted
Pig side, Riverside Cottages on the witch's house side.*]

VILLAGERS [*singing "The Street Song" while houses are wheeled in*]:

> If you want to keep your hands and arms,
> And your legs and knees and feet,
> Look to the right, look to the left,
> Look to the right again, look to the left again—
> *And then: don't cross the street!*

> CHORUS: Never cross the street,
>   Never cross the street.
>   If you want to claim your old-age pension,
>   Never cross the street in Street.

> If you want to keep a head that will think
> And a heart with a regular beat,
> Look to the right, look to the left, etc.

> *Repeat* CHORUS

> If life is your favourite habit,
> And death is not your treat,
> Look to the right, look to the left, etc.

> *Repeat* CHORUS

[*Traffic roar increases, then dies down as* LILY STEELE *runs in, blowing a shrill blast on her whistle. She is in her thirties, tough-looking, hair done in a tight bun, dressed in a navy gym tunic and black stockings.*]

LILY [*blowing whistle again*]: Hurry up, you lot! Street time! Street time!

[*As many* VILLAGERS *as possible line up in front of houses. They wear their luminous jackets and surgeons' masks. Wearing a black shawl,* MEG MIRKIN, *the official witch of Street, sits watching in wheelchair, front corner of stage.*]

LILY: Get a move on! You *know* we've only got five minutes, while the crossing gates are shut at Potash

Crossing East and Wilderness West. This is *our* time—
don't waste it!

[*Some of the crowd are inclined to scuffle. Shouts of
"Yah! Rotten Riverside rats!" "Boo! Filthy Forestside
pigs!" This may rise to a chant of "Up with the pigs,
down with the rats, We'll clobber them all with cricket
bats. Down with the horrible Forestside hicks, We'll knock
off their blocks with hockey sticks!"*]

LILY [*blowing whistle again sharply*]: Cut that out!
Father—belt up. I saw you try to trip Mr. Plout!

[FRED STEELE, *a big red-faced, white-haired man, landlord
of the Spotted Pig, looks abashed.*]

LILY: Come on—we only have five minutes a day, when
those level-crossing gates are closed—don't fool about.
We can't *afford* to. Remember how many people got
run over last week, Jenny Thatcher?

JENNY [*a thin teen-ager with crutches*]: Three, Lily.

LILY: Right. Two kids had broken legs and old Mr.
Deacon was killed. This is no time for politics. Get
going! Along the street and back. Each time I blow,
it's a twelve-foot truck passing you. Toomey Mirkin,
what's the drill?

TOOMEY [*He is a gentle, mild-looking boy, late teens.
He is noticeably lame. When he speaks,* JENNY THATCH-
ER *looks at him longingly and wistfully*]: Flatten!

LILY: Right—flatten! Ready—go!

[*They run along the street and back—i.e., upstage and
downstage—keeping to their own side of the street, flat-
tening against houses each time the whistle blows.*]

LILY [*blows whistle twice*]: Right! Now—Sue Thatcher

—there's a fourteen-foot juggernaut coming—what do you do?

SUE [*Jenny's mother—very tired, nervous-looking; she jumps when addressed*]: Er—get indoors, Lily!

[*laughter*]

LILY: If you can't?

SUE: Huddle!

LILY: Right—huddle! Down on your hip, in the angle of the wall. The wheels of a truck are its narrowest point. Ready—go!

[*They run as before. This time when she blows they fall flat—some of them with difficulty because of crutches, etc.—braced in the angle between wall and pavement.*]

LILY [*blows whistle*]: O-kay! Measurements! Father, two trucks coming opposite ways, one by the Spotted Pig, one by the post office, doing the usual fifty, where will they meet?

FRED: By the butcher's.

LILY: So get away from there. Meg Mirkin, truck coming round Baker's Corner with a load of adamite rods extending eight feet behind the truck's tailboard, whose house will they hit?

MEG [*bitterly*]: Mine.

[*Laughter, some shouts of "Serve you right, Riverside hag!"*]

LILY: Jenny Thatcher, you've a pram parked outside the baker's, trucks coming each way, what do you do?

JENNY: I shouldn't *have* a pram in the street.

LILY: Right. *Never* have a pram in the street. Hannah Steele—you see an old man fall in front of a truck— what do you do?

HANNAH [*taken by surprise. She and* TOOMEY *have been exchanging a long, intense look across the street. She is* LILY'*s sister, about* TOOMEY'*s age*]: Er—try to help him, Lily!

LILY: I'm *ashamed* of you—my own sister! *Never* try to help someone in the street. You can't do anything for them, and you only risk losing your own life. Okay—one more practice. If I blow once, it's flatten; twice, it's huddle. Ready—go!

[*They run again; some of them get muddled and bump each other. More scuffles and hostilities.* LILY *blows three times to indicate finish.* TOOMEY *and* HANNAH *try to get close enough to hold hands but are hustled to their respective sides of street.*]

LILY: Okay! Practice over! Stand by to receive milk and mail!

VILLAGERS [*singing*]:

> Here comes the heli-
> Here comes the heli-
> Here comes the heli-
>   copter, bringing milk and eggs
> And all the other deli-
> All the other deli-
> All the other deli-
>   cacies not supplied on legs,
> Bread and cheese and jelly,
> Tables, chairs, and telly,
> Books and bags and pegs.

> CHORUS: No one in Street has to bother to shop, a
>   Housewife in Street can take her ease.
>   All she requires is delivered by chopper,
>   All of life's little necessities!
>   Life is a treat, living's so sweet
>   In Street!

[*Noise of helicopter.* VILLAGERS *are lined along side of street, looking up. Rope descends from above with milkman's compartmented basket full of bottles. It travels up one side of street and down the other,* VILLAGERS *taking out bottles. Or they are passed from hand to hand. Groceries and mail are similarly distributed. Some shouts of* "Forestside pigs!" *and* "Riverside rats!" *while this is going on. As each person receives mail, he or she retires indoors —i.e., between houses. At last only* FRED *and* MEG *are left.*]

MEG [*calling across street*]: I'd like a word with you, Fred Steele.

FRED [*reading letter*]: I'm busy. Got no time for women's nattering. Specially an old Riverside bag.

MEG [*angrily*]: Will you please listen to me?

FRED [*reading*]: Sorry. No time.

MEG: Old Mr. Baker told me. [*He takes no notice; she repeats, louder.*] Old Mr. Baker had to go by ambulance to Ebbchester to get his foot X-rayed. [*At the mention of Ebbchester* FRED *looks up.*] And he says he saw you by the Market Cross, giving a bundle of money to one of the adamite truck drivers.

FRED [*sour and sharp*]: Old Baker wants his eyes examined, not his leg X-rayed. His sight's about as good as that of a myopic mole. [*defensively*] Anyway, how could he tell it was a truck driver I was talking to? Not that it's true, mind you.

MEG: He saw the man get into his truck. And he noticed the number: ADM 100. And that was the *same* truck, Fred Steele, that two days later crashed into Rose Carpenter's cottage and made it fall down.

FRED [*shrugging*]: So what? It happens all the time.

MEG: Old Mr. Baker said it looked deliberate.

FRED [*muttering*]: Old Mr. Baker better watch out or *he*'ll find himself under a truck.

MEG: How come, Fred Steele, it always happens on *our* side of the street, never on yours?

FRED [*shrugs again*]: Your houses are on the outside of the bend. The trucks' tails swing out. It's the luck of the game.

MEG: The luck of the game! There's more to it than that, Fred Steele. And I'm going to get to the bottom of it.

[*She wheels herself out of sight.*]

FRED [*vindictively*]: Meddlesome old besom! Call herself a witch! She'll get to the bottom of something else if she don't take care. Maybe it's time a truck skidded into *her* house. [*He stands scratching his head, looking after her. Then down at the letter in his hand. A smile spreads over his face. Then he bursts out laughing.*] So she thinks she's going to get to the bottom of it, does she? Wouldn't she get a shock if she knew who this letter was from? [*mocking, pantomiming*] Oh, by the way, Mrs. Mirkin, thought you'd like to know I'd heard from your boy Hannibal, that ran away all those long years ago. [*reflective, reminiscent*] Your naughty boy Hannibal, what stole the key of the toll bridge.

[*Lights dim; streetlights shine.* FRED *is now in shadow.* TOOMEY *and* HANNAH *appear on balconies on respective sides of street. They signal to each other with regular gestures, as if talking in deaf-and-dumb language, and sing, so it can be assumed they are communicating through signs.*]

TOOMEY [*singing*]:

I love you from the window and I love you from the street,
In wintry cold or sleet,
In summer's dust and heat.
I love you but I can't imagine how we'll ever meet.
We'll never never, never never meet.

HANNAH [*singing*]:

I love you through the window and I love you through the
    wall.
During all that may befall,
I'll love you best of all,
But oh, my love, I don't believe we'll ever meet at all.
I don't believe we'll ever meet at all!

BOTH:

I love you more than sun or moon or cheese with apple
    tart.
I will give you all my heart
For I'm pierced by Cupid's dart,
But oh, my dearest angel, we are doomed to live apart.
My dearest, we are doomed to live apart.

FRED [*very angry*]: You little hussy! Carrying on with a
Riversider! I'll lock you in the beer cellar for that.
We'll see if twelve hours shut inside a barrel will make
you sing a different tune. Lily! Take her down to the
cellar!

[LILY *appears behind* HANNAH *and collars her.*]

HANNAH [*terrified*]: Oh, no, Father! Oh, please, Lily!
[*She is dragged off.*]

[VILLAGERS *in surgeons' masks appear and shout at*
TOOMEY.]

VILLAGERS: Ought to be ashamed of yourself, Toomey
Mirkin—taking up with Fred Steele's daughter. Shame!
Boo! Keep to your own side! Stay where you belong!

How dare you flirt with someone on the other side of the street?

[*Lights dim. Traffic noise intensifies.*]

[BLACKOUT]

SCENE TWO

Lights go up to show that the Thatcher house frame has been reversed and placed centre stage to suggest interior. SUE, *careworn and jumpy, is pressing a tutu on ironing board with old-fashioned flatiron.* JENNY *is lying on floor, doing homework with exercise book and bottle of ink. She has a plaster cast or bandage on one leg. Traffic noise, at first loud roar, diminishes to just-audible rumble, alternated with occasional shriek of brakes or loud crash. When this happens,* SUE *jumps nervously, sometimes puts her hands to her ears. Once she drops the iron. At one loud screech of brakes* JENNY *goes to the side of screen to look past it and speaks.*

JENNY: Old Mr. Baker got run over.

[SUE *presses her lips together.*]

SUE [*sharply*]: Get on with your homework!

VOICES [*outside*]: Ought to be ashamed of yourself, Toomey Mirkin! Boo!

JENNY: *Why* can't Toomey love Hannah?

SUE: Don't be stupid. You can't love someone on the other side of the street.

JENNY [*softly*]: But suppose you can't help it?

SUE: Iron's cold. [*Ignoring* JENNY's *question, she goes out.*]

JENNY [*singing very quietly and simply*]:

> *I* love *him*,
> *He* loves *her*,
> That is how
> These things occur.

> Why does this
> Have to be?
> Why, oh why
> Can't *he* love *me*?

> It would give
> Me such joy
> If she'd love some
> Other boy.

> Which might then
> Leave him free
> Just to take a
> Look at *me*.

> Oh, what sad
> Geometry!
> A loves B and
> B loves C.

> Such are Love's
> Spiteful spells.
> Why can't B love
> Someone else?

[*spoken*] *But!*
[*singing again*]:

> *He* loves *her*.
> *She* loves *him*.
> So my outlook's
> Rather grim.

[*sung very softly and resignedly*]:

> *I* love *him*.
> *He* loves *her*.
> That's the way
> These things occur.

[*Sue returns with fresh iron.* JENNY *goes on with her homework, absently whistling the tune of the song.*]

SUE [*outburst of rage*]: *Stop* that whistling, will you! It goes through and through my head! I'll give you such a clip—

JENNY [*gives nervous start*]: Sorry, Mother.

[*Another loud bang outside.*]

SUE: *Oh,* this traffic! It's enough to drive you mad.

JENNY: It isn't any worse than usual, is it?

SUE [*hopelessly*]: Maybe not. Maybe it's just my nerves. [*ironing*] Sometimes it seems impossible to *believe* that it hasn't always been like this.

JENNY: What was it like when you were young, Mum?

SUE: Quiet. Peaceful. No traffic in the street. Kids could play *games* there—like with marbles and balls and skipping ropes.

JENNY: What are skipping ropes?

SUE [*pause, glance at* JENNY]: What's a *skipping rope?* Oh, well, I suppose it's no use trying to explain. Wouldn't be much use to you. [*sighing*] And then— every spring—there was the Bull Fair.

JENNY: What happened?

SUE: I've told you, dozens of times.

JENNY: Tell me again.

SUE: All the wild bulls would be rounded up that had roamed out of the forest and spent the winter on the salt marshes. And then they'd let them run loose through the street.

JENNY: Wasn't it dangerous?

SUE: *Dangerous?* Compared with the way it is now? Well, of course the old people—children—anyone who couldn't run fast—would watch from their windows. The village witch would go out to greet the King Bull. And all the boys would run in front. Like a race, it was. I remember once—

[*Loud bang outside. A photograph in frame falls from above and breaks.*]

SUE [*cry of anguish*]: Oh! It's the photo of your granny. I *knew* I shouldn't hang it up. *Nothing's* safe on the wall any more.

JENNY [*terrified, placating, as if she were used to being blamed for all breakages*]: Never mind, Mum! The picture's all right. It's only the glass that's broke. I'll get the dustpan.

[*She hobbles out.*]

[SUE *blows dust off photo and lays it on ironing board; gives last touch to her ironing and shakes out tutu.*]

JENNY [*returning with dustpan and brush, kneels awkwardly to sweep up the glass*]: What were you going to say about the bulls, Mum?

SUE [*dully*]: I forget. Anyway, everything's different now. The marsh is all covered with waste from the adamite mines. And the bulls have gone back into the forest.

JENNY [*dreamily*]: And instead of bulls in the street, there are trucks. I wish I'd seen one of the Bull Fairs.

SUE: And all the people on our side of the street hate the ones living on the other side.

JENNY: Why should we hate the Mirkins? They're our cousins. [*softly*] I don't hate Toomey Mirkin.

SUE [*irritable*]: Oh, we just do. You're bound to hate people you can't ever talk to. [*wistfully*] I haven't spoken to Meg in years. Haven't talked to Toomey since he was a little fellow.

[*Another bang outside.* SUE *jumps and steps backward, knocking over* JENNY'*s ink.*]

JENNY [*dismayed*]: *Oh*—all over my sums—

SUE [*furious*]: *How* many times have I told you, you *stupid*, stupid, careless girl, *not* to leave unstoppered ink on the floor?

[*She slaps* JENNY, *who drops the brush and pan she was holding.* SUE *angrily sweeps up the glass while* JENNY *cries, silently and wretchedly.* SUE *takes out the dustpan and returns with a cloth; seeing* JENNY, *she is stricken with remorse.*]

SUE [*putting her arm round* JENNY, *who at first flinches nervously*]: There, there, dearie! I didn't mean to hit you. [*passionately*] I don't *ever* mean to hit you—it's just something that comes over me because of those blasted everlasting trucks. The noise goes through and through my head till I don't know what I'm *doing* . . . don't cry! I didn't mean to scold you. *Specially* on your birthday! Look, your present's finished. [*holds up tutu*] Want to try it on?

JENNY [*rubbing away tears, smiling nervously*]: Oh, yes! Oh, it's beautiful, Mum. [*She wraps tutu round her and slips off jeans; her injured leg is now even more obvi-*

ous.] Thank you, Mother—it's just what I've always wanted! [*hesitantly*] If only I could have dancing lessons too—

SUE: *Dancing* lessons? Going into Ebbchester by helicopter? Are you out of your mind? Do you think we're millionaires? [*sighing*] To think that when I was young there was a bus every hour—every *day*—and it only cost eightpence return. And you could walk across the street whenever you wanted to do a bit of shopping.

JENNY [*In spite of her bad leg she is bravely attempting to take up ballet attitudes, leaning on the ironing board.*]: But what happened? When did it all change?

SUE: Well, you know there used to be a toll bridge down at the bottom of the street? [JENNY *nods.*] And old Mr. Mirkin—

JENNY [*wistfully*]: Toomey's father?

SUE: That's right. He owned the bridge, and he only used to let twenty cars across every hour. So the ones that were in a hurry went a long way round.

JENNY [*hopping along the ironing board*]: Yes? Then what happened?

SUE: Toomey's elder brother, Hannibal, stole the key of the bridge.

[BLACKOUT]

SCENE THREE

Houses are removed. A hamburger stand is wheeled in, which has a sign on one side in large letters: Hannibal's Hamburgers. There is a coffee machine, buns, Coke tins, soft-drink bottles. Towards front of stage a signpost with two arms. One says STREET, 40 miles. The other says ADAMITE MINES, 40 miles.

HANNIBAL *has been inspecting the stall, running finger over surface for dust, poking buns, etc. Now he is drinking a cup of coffee. He is in his thirties, fat, flashy, complacent. Smokes cigar.* BERT, *who runs the stall, is an oldish man, anxious about his job.*

While scenery is changed, VILLAGERS *at stage front sing.*

VILLAGERS [*singing*]:

> Hannibal's burgers are flat and tough.
> One in a lifetime is quite enough.
> Apart from the taste and the sheer expense,
> They're packed to the brim with carcinogens.

> CHORUS: Olé, olé, oh lummy, olé,
> Don't let's have Hannibalburgers today.

> Hannibalburgers are red as ruby.
> Only a blind, besotted booby
> Would ever suspend his disbelief
> Enough to assume they were made of beef.

> *Repeat* CHORUS

> Swallow the bun at a single gulp.
> It's made from coloured inflated pulp,
> A mixture of softwood and Styrofoam.
> Oh, what a feast for a gastronome!

> *Repeat* CHORUS

> Hannibalburgers are made from blubber,
> Polythene bags, and cable rubber,
> Insulation from telephone wires,
> And miles of minced-up bicycle tyres.

> *Repeat* CHORUS

BERT [*ringing handbell and shouting*]: Hannibal's hamburgers! Hannibal's all-fresh hamburgers!

[*Sound of brakes. Cab of truck appears. License number ADM 100. Driver walks in.*]

DRIVER: Give us a coffee, Bert.

HANNIBAL [*as Bert fills paper cup with coffee*]: You not having a hamburger?

DRIVER: Not likely. Nor would you if you knew what was in 'em. Up around the adamite mines they'll tell you those hamburgers is made from mountain rats. That's how Hannibal got to be a millionaire.

BERT [*has been making desperate attempts to catch the driver's eye, winking and grimacing*]: Hey, mate, you want to watch what you say. That's libel, that is.

DRIVER [*shrugging*]: Can't be libel if it's the truth, can it? Two pound a hundred, he was paying for rats.

BERT: Watch your tongue, mate—strewth!

HANNIBAL [*laughing heartily*]: Don't stop him, Bert! That just shows the grapevine gets things half right. [*to driver*] I happen to *be* Hannibal. And I can tell you it's absolutely true about the mountain rats—except that when they ran short, we had to fall back on weasels and foxes.

DRIVER [*apprehensive, suspicious*]: Er—cripes—you really *are* Hannibal?

[*Hannibal nods, beaming.*]

DRIVER: And is it true, then, about the million you made from these bars?

HANNIBAL: Nah. Only half a million. But then I bought my way into the adamite mines. Did all right. Now I'm going home to the peaceful little village I came from long ago. [*sentimentally*] To my little brother and my dear old mother and the roses round the door.

BERT [*sycophantically sentimental*]: Ahh! Where's that then, where you come from, Mr. Hannibal?

HANNIBAL: Why, it's a little village called Street. Know it? About—[*he turns to consult signpost*]—it's about forty miles from here.

BERT: Arr! That's where they used to hold them Bull Fairs, in the old days, wannit? Race through the streets with bulls and all that? They do that when you were a boy, Mr. Hannibal?

[*Hannibal looks annoyed. He does not reply.*]

DRIVER: Sure, that's the place. *I* know Street. Drive through there three times a week with a load of adamite from the mines. As a matter o' fact—[*he stops rather suddenly, looking sorry he started, and adds after a moment*]—I reckon you won't find it quite so peaceful nowadays.

HANNIBAL: Oh? Why? Has it grown?

DRIVER: *Grown?* No, it's not *grown.*

BERT: Nowhere for it *to* grow, is there? River on one side, where the bridge is. And that big wall on the other, that goes all round the forest. That's why it's called Street, ennit? 'Cos a street's all it is, just about.

DRIVER: And a heck of a lot of traffic along it. [*to* HANNIBAL] I daresay in your day the toll bridge was still there? In those days the through traffic went fifty miles round, by Fordham and Marshfield. But as soon as the toll bridge was done away with and the new bridge built, all the adamite trucks started going through. It was quicker, see?

HANNIBAL [*complacently*]: Sure. I know all about the toll bridge. *I* fixed that.

BERT [*fake admiration*]: *You* did, Mr. Hannibal? How'd you do that, then?

HANNIBAL [*laughing*]: My old dad inherited the bridge from *his* dad. Used to stand by the toll gate collecting pennies. Fourpence for a loaded wagon or truck, it was. Twopence for a car, penny a motorcycle. Halfpenny for a pushbike. Pedestrians free. But when I left home, I took the key of the bridge with me! [*He pauses for applause. Both men look at him in silence.*] Sold it to a construction company. They got that new bridge up in six weeks flat.

BERT: *You* did that?

HANNIBAL [*nodding*]: That was how I got the capital to start my burger business. *Imagine* it—Dad would only let twenty cars an hour through! He said that was enough—the others could go some other way. [*as the other two remain silent, he adds defensively*] After all, it was only a grotty, narrow old bridge. You can't hold up progress.

BERT: O' *course* you can't, Mr. Hannibal! Progress has to—to pro*gress*, dunnit? Can't help it if somebody's corns gets run over in the process.

DRIVER [*much interested*]: And this is the first time you've been back to Street since you left? [HANNIBAL nods.]

How long is that, then?

HANNIBAL: Matter of seventeen years. Used to be a niceish pub there—the Spotted Pig. I was going steady with the landlord's daughter—Lily Steele—*she*'ll be a bit long in the tooth now. [*He laughs.*] Hmm. [*reminiscently*] Lily Steele—she was a tough judy even then. You finished your coffee, bud? Then you could give me a lift in your truck along to Street.

BERT [*amazed*]: You got a million put away, boss, and you're asking for a *lift*?

DRIVER [*equally surprised*]: Why, they got helicopter services to Street nowadays, only no one can't afford the fare, *and* daily milk deliveries by chopper; I often nobble a couple o' pints out o' the basket as I go through. [*grinning*]

HANNIBAL [*peevishly*]: I don't wish to go by helicopter. I've a notion to go back and surprise them all—arrive on foot, just the way I left. [*to himself*] They used to laugh at me. They won't do *that* any more. [*to driver*] You drop me by the Spotted Pig, that'll do me. I'll just fetch my bag. [*He goes out.*]

DRIVER [*indignant*]: I'm not giving *him* any lift. What a rotten swine! Pinched his dad's livelihood—and what he did has just about *wrecked* that place. *I* wouldn't live there—not if it was the last town in the country. They get a truck through every thirty seconds. You can't get to the other side of the street! Here, I'm leaving before he gets back—there's ten for the coffee, Bert.

BERT [*alarmed*]: Hey, you better watch it, mate. He can be real horrible when he's crossed. In the firm we call him Hatchet Hannibal—he'll sack a bloke if he don't like the colour of his hair.

DRIVER: That so? I'm off then.

BERT: Wait, I got a message for you from Fred Steele. He says thanks for the thatched-house job, and now, will you knock a few chips off the next one—blue paint, diamond panes. Here's ten quid. And he says he can't meet you no more in Ebbchester—somebody saw him. He'll be in touch. [*Hands over money.*]

DRIVER: Okay. Ta.

BERT [*meditatively*]: Bit of a lousy trick, ennit? Bash people's houses on purpose?

DRIVER [*carefree*]: Oh, it's only empty ones. Mr. Steele tells me which they are—it's to make the council get a move on and condemn them. [*low voice*] Oh, cripes—here comes Fatso.

HANNIBAL [*reappearing with tartan bag*]: Right, I'm ready.

DRIVER: Sorry, guvnor, I can't give you a lift. Not supposed to take passengers, you know. It's as much as my job's worth.

HANNIBAL [*ominously*]: It'd be as much as your job was worth *not* to take me. I'm a friend of your boss.

DRIVER [*wildly*]: But, look, guv—*honest*—it ain't a bit of *use* my giving you a lift. I can't *stop* in Street. The traffic won't *allow* you to stop—let alone there's no place to park. You might as well ask for a lift to the middle of Niagara *Falls*.

BERT [*placatingly*]: He's right, you know, boss. Tell you what—there's a bike in my shed someone left here. Why don't you take that? Here, I'll get it [*he does so*]; see, you could put your bag on the carrier—and I'll just give the tyres a bit of a pump.

[*While he is doing this, the* DRIVER *unobtrusively leaves.*]

HANNIBAL [*annoyed*]: Oh, all right.

BERT [*triumphantly*]: Well, you said you wanted to return 'umbly, didn't you, guv?

[HANNIBAL *mounts the bike and rides out rather insecurely.*]

[BLACKOUT]

SCENE FOUR

While scene is changed, groups of VILLAGERS *at either side of stage shout insults at one another.*

FORESTSIDERS: Yah! Boo! Dirty Riverside rats. Let's throw stink bombs at the Riverside rats. Riverside rats —eat from their hats—spit on their mats—carve up their cats; we—hate—Riverside rats. Let's shoot poisoned darts at them!

RIVERSIDERS: Hoo! Boo! Forestside pigs—all wear wigs—chew their cigs—are horrible prigs—take syrup of figs; we—loathe—the Forestside pigs. Let's throw stink bombs at them!

[*Darts and stink bombs are exchanged. Then they retire. The street is now reassembled, with the Mirkin house frame in centre, reversed to show interior side, which has a fireplace with mantelpiece painted on it. Props include a kitchen table with drawer, a vegetable rack containing a glass witch ball, an old hand mangle, and a basket of bricks.*

MEG *is sitting in her wheelchair wrapped in a black shawl. She holds a black walking stick.*]

MEG: By the power of Nimmuz, Thimmuz, and Grimmuz! By Belial, Asmodelius, and Agrippa! By Ashteroth, Fishteroth, and Balliol—staff, make the fire burn! Staff, make the mangle turn.

[*She holds out the staff. Nothing happens.*]

MEG [*angry and worried*]: By Nimrod, Slimrod, and
Elginbrod! By Nero, Pharaoh, and Zero! *Make* the
mangle turn! *Make* the fire burn! [*Nothing happens.*]
Magic wand, in my hand, please obey, what I say!
[*Nothing happens.*]

MEG [*furious, becoming desperate*]: By Hansel and Gretel
and Popocatepetl! Make the fire *explode*, if you want
to! Make the table stand on one leg! Just *do* it—that's
all I ask, *do* it! [*Nothing happens.*] Oh, all right! Rot
you, then! May you be riddled from end to end with
woodworm, dry rot, and deathwatch beetle.

[*She throws the stick down furiously. After a moment she
is sorry and leans forward to try to get it back, but it is out
of reach.*]

MEG: Wand, come here. I'm sorry I lost my temper.
Come here. By Nimmuz, Thimmuz, and Grimmuz,
wand, wand, come to my hand. [*The wand remains
motionless.*] Damn you, *will* you do as I say? [*The wand
does not move.*] Oh! [*She buries her face in her hands.*]
Oh, I've lost the knack, I've lost it! What shall I do,
what ever shall I do?

[*Sound of door banging.* MEG *instantly composes herself.*
TOOMEY *limps in.*]

MEG: D'you want some supper?

TOOMEY: Is there any milk?

MEG: It didn't come today. I think that truck driver
pinched it again.

TOOMEY: Never mind. D'you want me to light the fire?
[*She shakes her head. He goes towards table.*]

MEG [*trying to be casual*]: Oh—Toomey—could you pass
me my magic wand?

[*Looking surprised, he does so, then sits on table, hangs basket of bricks over his lame leg, and proceeds to exercise it by hoisting basket up and down. Traffic noise begins outside. A cup falls from above and breaks after a very loud rumble.*]

MEG: There goes the last of my wedding china. Good thing your father's not here. It's thirteen years next Friday since the truck killed him.

TOOMEY [*sighing*]: Try not to think about it, Mother.

MEG: What *else* is there to think about? Only you and me left out of the whole family. And the traffic's so bad that I can't even cross the street to quarrel with my own sister-in-law. Haven't had a word with Sue Thatcher in years. . . . and [*in a low voice*—TOOMEY *doesn't hear*] something's gone wrong with my magic.

TOOMEY [*after a minute or two*]: Maybe the traffic will improve. They say the adamite in the mines will be exhausted someday.

MEG: Not in my lifetime.

TOOMEY: Maybe the bypass will get built.

MEG: What a hope! There's too much hate in the village. Nobody'd ever agree on where it was to go. Why— Fred Steele—and all the people who live on the Forest-side—want to put it *here*. Where *our* houses are. [*to herself*] And I'm sure Fred Steele is paying truck drivers to bash houses on this side. [*shaking wand angrily*] And I can't stop him!

TOOMEY [*who has not been attending. Puts down basket and limps to face* MEG]: Mother, there's something I've got to tell you.

MEG: What is it, Toomey? Your leg hurting again? [*She*

makes a move to touch it with her stick. Restrains herself.]

TOOMEY: No. It's getting better. It isn't that. Mother— I want to marry Hannah Steele.

MEG: *What?*

TOOMEY: I want to marry Hannah Steele.

MEG [*after pause*]: Are you crazy?

TOOMEY: I love her. And she loves me. We want to get married.

MEG: But you live on opposite sides of the *street*! You've never even *met*.

TOOMEY: We see each other from our windows. We talk. In sign language. We love each other.

MEG [*more and more appalled*]: Do you realize who that girl *is*?

[TOOMEY *nods repeatedly, as if he felt he knew better than anyone else in the world.*]

MEG: Her sister Lily is the one your brother Hannibal was engaged to—before he ran off with the key to the toll bridge. He *jilted* Lily—and she's never married anyone else. Maybe she still pines for Hannibal.

TOOMEY: I don't see how she could. [*detachedly*] He was horrible.

MEG: And her father—Fred Steele—hates us like *poison*! He's the chairman of the Forestsiders. He'd rather push you under a truck than let you marry his younger daughter.

TOOMEY [*gentle, obstinate*]: But I *love* Hannah.

MEG: Honestly, my dear—you'll just *have* to put her out of your mind.

TOOMEY: But Mother—you're the witch—you've got your wand. [*She looks at it and shrugs.*] Can't you help us? Can't you think of *something*? [*She shakes her head.*] Can't you look in your glass ball and see some way out for us? Please?

MEG: It won't be any use. The ball has been as black as ink—the last few times I've looked in it.

TOOMEY: Please try.

MEG: Oh, very well. It won't help. But bring it here. [*He takes the ball from the vegetable rack, but as he is passing it to her there is a tremendous crash outside, which makes them both start; the ball slips from their hands, falls, and breaks.*]

TOOMEY [*in horror*]: Oh, Ma! Your magic ball!

MEG [*resignedly*]: It didn't work, anyway. Nothing works any more.

TOOMEY: What about your ring? Your serpent's-egg ring? Wouldn't that help in some way?

MEG [*Brings her left hand from under shawl; she wears a ring with a huge flashing green stone.*]: No—the ring won't work for me either. I can't help you, Toomey. [*after a pause, during which the rumble of traffic changes to shriek of brakes, giving way to shouts and commotion*] If I had any power left, don't you think I would have done something about the way things *are*? [*bitterly*]

[*They both remain gloomily silent.*]

MEG [*briskly*]: What was that awful crash, anyway?

[TOOMEY *hobbles to side of screen and looks out as from window.*]

TOOMEY: Can't make out—people in the way. Oh, I

think it's poor little Jenny Thatcher—yes, I can see
Mrs. Thatcher, she's very upset. They're trying to move
the kid—I think—I'm afraid—she's very badly hurt—
it was one of those big adamite trucks—filthy rotten
brutes—the truck's jammed right across the street.

MEG [*sad, reflective*]: Jenny Thatcher. My own niece.
And I've hardly ever spoken to her—though she lives
just across the street. You'd think she'd had enough
bad luck already—poor child.

[*There is a loud rat-tat, or ring of doorbell, and* LILY
strides in. MEG *and* TOOMEY *are amazed to see her.*]

MEG: *Lily Steele?*

TOOMEY: Lily Steele?

MEG: How did you get across the street?

LILY [*coldly*]: There's a truck jammed cornerways on.
The one that hit the Thatcher girl. It'll take them ten
minutes to shift it. All the traffic's come to a stop.

MEG [*eyes widen as idea strikes her*]: Oh! I could go and
say a word to poor Sue Thatcher.

LILY: No! Don't you go! I've got something to say to
you two.

MEG [*composedly, but she is tense*]: Well? What is it?

LILY: First, there's a message from Dad. To you. [*ad-
dressing* TOOMEY] If he catches you making any more
signals to our Hannah, he's going to shoot you with
his crossbow and a poison dart. And he's a dead shot,
Dad is. Get it? Hannah's not for *you*—you rotten little
Riverside rat!

TOOMEY [*firmly*]: I love her. And she loves me.

LILY: I don't suppose she loves you much at the moment.

She's shut up inside an empty beer barrel, thanks to you.

TOOMEY: How *dare* you? How dare you treat her so? You're monsters! I'll get her away somehow—and I'll marry her.

LILY: Are you kidding? After what that brother of yours did to this village? [*to* MEG] You must be very proud of your son Hannibal! As for *this* one—Dad would see him at the bottom of the river before he'd let him marry Hannah. Why—he hasn't even got two good *legs*.

TOOMEY: Just the same I *shall* marry her—you'll see.

MEG [*simultaneously*]: That wasn't a very kind thing to say. There are plenty of people in Street with a broken leg—or two—like me.

LILY: Well, if you want to keep him—broken leg and all—advise him to keep away from Hannah. Otherwise —phttt! [*She makes poison-dart gesture.*]

[*Doorbell rings again—or knocker.*]

VILLAGER'S VOICE: Mrs. Mirkin! Mrs. Mirkin!

[*A* VILLAGER *comes in, wearing luminous roadman's jacket.*]

VILLAGER: Mrs. Mirkin, Mrs. Thatcher asks if you will kindly come and use your power on her daughter Jenny, who has been hit by a truck and is likely to die.

MEG [*sounding very tired*]: No. Just tell her no. I'm sorry. There's nothing I can do.

VILLAGER [*outraged*]: *Nothing?* You can't do nothing —for your own *niece*?

MEG [*quietly*]: Nothing. I can't help Jenny. [*The* VILLAGER *goes out.* MEG *glances at* LILY, *then at* TOOMEY.] Toomey—would you be kind enough to go and explain to Susan Thatcher that—just that I can't help her. [*bitterly*] Heaven knows I would if I could.

[TOOMEY *nods and limps out.* MEG *looks after him, then turns back to* LILY.]

MEG: Well, Lily Steele? That wasn't the only thing you came to say—was it?

LILY [*partly defiant, partly taken aback, recognizing* MEG's *powerful personality*]: No. No . . . that *wasn't* all.

[BLACKOUT]

SCENE FIVE

Lights go up to reveal group of VILLAGERS *kneeling in front of stage against backdrop. People are supporting the injured* JENNY. *Some are restraining* SUE, *who would like to hurl herself at the* TRUCK DRIVER.

SUE: You bloody murderer! Going through the village at seventy— *Look* what you've done! It was her *birthday*. She just slipped next door to show her new dress to Lucy. *Let* me get at him, I'll tear his eyes out—

VILLAGERS: Hold on—easy, girl, easy—it wasn't the poor beggar's fault—gently now, missus.

DRIVER [*aggrievedly*]: *Course* it wasn't my fault—traffic was pushing along, I couldn't *go* no slower—she shoulda kept in closer against the wall.

SUE: I'd like to *kill* you—

DRIVER [*with one hand over his eye, which is blackened*]: Well, you damn nearly done that already. What a tartar!

SUE [*weeping*]: Oh, my Lord! I used to hit Jenny so *often* —when the traffic got on my nerves. Jenny—Jen— *don't die!* [*She kneels by* JENNY.] Jenny, speak to me. [*frantically*]

VILLAGER: Hey—why don't we fetch the witch?

ANOTHER: Yeah—why not get old Meg Mirkin? She might be able to do something for the kid. I'll get her. [*He goes out.*]

SUE [*calls after him*]: Oh, what's the use? Meg can't do anything. She's lost her power.

FIRST VILLAGER: Yeah, I reckon that's true. Since she got run over she can't do no more magic. Lost the touch.

SUE [*pleadingly*]: Jen? Is there anything you'd like? Anything I can get you?

JENNY [*very faint*]: Yes—I'd like to speak to Toomey Mirkin.

VILLAGERS [*surprised*]: Toomey Mirkin? Meg's boy? What'd she want to say to *him*? Cousins, aren't they? Yeah, but they live on opposite sides of the street. Funny she'd want to see *him*. Hey—look, here he comes.

TOOMEY [*comes in and limps up to* SUE]: Aunt Susan? Mother asked me to tell you that—that she's very sorry, but she can't do anything for Jenny. She's *very* sorry.

VILLAGERS [*awestruck whispers*]: Oo, did you hear that? Says she can't do nothing! Well, she mighta come *herself*! That's as good as admitting she's not a proper witch any longer. Poor little Jenny—you'd think she mighta *tried*, at least—wouldn't have hurt her to come out.

SUE [*standing up, with dignity*]: Thank you, Toomey.

Will you tell my sister-in-law that I—I am sorry she
didn't see fit—I'm sorry she couldn't help? [*She swallows
and takes control of herself.*] As you *are* here, Toomey
—Jenny would like a word with you.

TOOMEY: *Jenny?* I thought she—of course. [*He goes
and kneels by* JENNY, *awkwardly. She looks up and
gestures to him to put his head right down by her.*]

[*While they remain in this position the* VILLAGERS *sing
mournfully.*]

VILLAGERS [*singing*]:

Poor Jenny lies a-sleeping, a-sleeping, a-sleeping,
Poor Jenny lies a-sleeping in the bright summer sun.
Poor Jenny lies a-sleeping, a-sleeping, a-sleeping,
Poor Jenny lies a-sleeping, her troubles are done.

VILLAGER [*shouting*]: Right away now! We got 'er
going again.

[*Traffic roar starts up. Several* VILLAGERS *carry out* JENNY.
Everybody else goes out.]

[BLACKOUT]

SCENE SIX

The Mirkins' kitchen as before. MEG *and* LILY *are still
confronting each other in exactly the same attitudes.*

LILY: Look here, Meg Mirkin. That properly showed
you up—didn't it? You couldn't do anything for that
poor kid. You're no good at your job any more—*are*
you? You've not done a thing for anyone in the village
—since I can remember! You've not done any incanta-

tions—or cast any runes—or cured anybody—or even *cursed* anybody! You're *useless*!

[MEG *makes halfhearted gesture with her wand; desists, waiting.*]

MEG: Well?

LILY: It's time you handed over to somebody else.

MEG: Meaning you?

LILY: Yes! Meaning me! *I* could cast spells—get things done—you give me that wand!

[*She moves forward a step.* MEG *deliberately breaks wand.*]

LILY: Hah! You can't get out of it *that* way. There's still the ring—the serpent's-egg ring.

MEG [*Her hand has been under her shawl. She pulls it out. The ring shines. They both look at it.*]: The ring—goes to whom I choose. I shall give it to my son's—to Toomey's wife.

LILY: What about your elder son? What about Hannibal? What about the thieving cheat who stole the bridge key and went off, promising me he'd be back in a month? *I'd* be *his* wife if—if he was here. *I* ought to have that ring! Give it to me!

MEG: No.

[LILY *makes a hostile move, but* MEG *gives her a look that daunts her.*]

MEG: Hannibal left the village. The ring goes to Toomey's wife.

LILY: That little cripple won't marry. [*She makes a snatch at the ring—but she is nervous.* MEG *puts her hand back under the shawl.*] *You* can't use it—can you? Any more than you could use your wand. I *know*

you can't. And I know why, too. Go on! *Do* something!
Call up a couple of Druids! Turn me into a snake. I
dare you!

MEG: No.

LILY: I dare you! I dare you!

MEG: The ring is the badge of office. It should not be
used for spite—for unimportant, petty tricks.

LILY [*talking to distract* MEG's *attention as she edges
sideways*]: Unimportant! And what do you think *is*
important, then? You don't think it's important that no
one in this village can get to the other side of the street
any more?

MEG [*listening to traffic, which has started up again*]:
They've got the traffic going. You can't get back now.
You'll have to wait here till next street-exercise time—
or walk twenty miles to Ebbchester and cross at their
zebra and walk back the other side.

LILY: I don't care! I'm *sick* of home—serving in the bar
—listening to Dad go on and on about how he'd get a
bypass put in if he had a bit more cash to grease up
the chaps on the County Council.

MEG: Oh? And just exactly where does he plan to put
the bypass?

LILY: Dunno. Through the forest, I suppose.

[*They both glance superstitiously, apprehensively, back-
wards.*]

MEG: The *forest*? He *couldn't*. It's all protected. Belongs
to the Historic Trust.

LILY: Let them part with a bit of it, then.

MEG: It's the only bit of prehistoric forest left in Europe.

The wild white cattle have lived undisturbed in it since before the Romans came.

LILY: Time they *were* disturbed.

MEG: They were driven out of the marshes—out of the village. The forest is all they have left. All the wild power that used to be dispersed over the whole country is now concentrated in the forest. If *that* was destroyed—

[*She has forgotten to keep her eye on* LILY, *who has been moving round behind her chair. Now* LILY *pounces, grabs* MEG's *wrist, and pulls the ring off her finger—puts it on her own.*]

LILY [*triumphantly*]: *Got* it! Fooled you, Meg Mirkin! *Now* you'll see!

[*Light on* LILY *makes the ring flash.*]

MEG [*not too discomposed*]: Well? What will I see? What will you do now, Lily Steele?

LILY: First I'll wish for Hannibal to come home. [*She stands in attitude of command, clenched fists raised.*]

MEG [*dryly*]: *That's* your notion of getting things done for the village?

LILY [*disregarding her*]: And when he *does* come, I'll curse him! I'll curse him for the seventeen wasted years. I'll say, "Hannibal Mirkin—"

MEG: My poor Lily. There's more to being witch of Street than just having the serpent's-egg ring on your finger. It will only work for its proper master, you know.

LILY [*shouting*]: What do you know about it, you stupid old cow? We'll soon see about that.

[TOOMEY *comes in, behind* LILY. *He is somewhat changed since his interview with the dying* JENNY. *He looks grave and more mature. He sees the ring on* LILY's *finger, moves quietly round behind her, and grabs her by her bun, which undoes into two plaits; he winds them into the mangle.*]

LILY [*furious*]: Oh! Let me go! Damn you, let me go! [*She can't move.* TOOMEY *takes the ring and hands it back to* MEG, *who puts it on.*]

MEG: Thank you, Toomey. She couldn't really have done any harm with it.

LILY [*raging*]: Oh, couldn't I? Couldn't I? What do you know about it? Just you wait!

[*Noise outside swells to a terrific chorus of catcalls and boos.* HANNIBAL *comes in, wheeling bike, the front wheel of which is broken. He looks rather startled and dishevelled. He leans the bike against the table and puts down his bag.*]

HANNIBAL: Well, well! Back in the old home! Hullo, Mother! [*He gives* MEG *a perfunctory kiss. Does not see* LILY, *who is behind him. But she watches him with a look of triumph.*]

MEG [*after a pause*]: Why, it's Hannibal. Come back— after all these years. [*She does not sound overjoyed.*]

HANNIBAL [*glancing round casually*]: Is this Toomey? Not grown much, have you? Where's Father?

MEG [*expressionless*]: Your father was run over by a truck—a long time ago.

HANNIBAL [*recollecting*]: Oh, that's right, Fred Steele did say—[*he checks himself*] how about little Mary?

MEG: She was run over too.

HANNIBAL: The old dog—Chico?

TOOMEY: Run over.

MEG [*dryly*]: It didn't sound as if you were getting much of a welcome out there.

HANNIBAL [*easily*]: Oh, a few rounds of drinks in the Spotted Pig will soon put that right.

TOOMEY: How are you going to get across to the Spotted Pig?

HANNIBAL [*exuberant, taking no notice of* TOOMEY]: I'm a rich man now, Mother! Made a pile up there in the mining district. Now I've got lots of plans. I'm coming back here to live—going to liven up the old place till you won't recognize it.

MEG: Indeed?

HANNIBAL: I must have a chat with old Fred Steele. I see he's the chairman of the County Council. [*pulling out local paper from his pocket*] Picture of him in here with his daughter—very pretty girl! That wouldn't be *Lily*? She must be getting pretty weathered by now, and she was never any oil painting; this must be the younger one—what was *her* name—Hannah? [*He glances about the room discontentedly.*] What a pokey little place this is! I'd forgotten it was so small and dark. [*Crosses to mantelpiece.*] Why are all the ornaments nailed on here?

TOOMEY: To stop them falling off. The traffic shakes them.

[MEG *signals to* TOOMEY. *He silently releases* LILY *from the mangle. She looks at* HANNIBAL *with clenched fists; he is rummaging in his bag for a cigar, which he lights. She silently goes out. Bang of door.*]

HANNIBAL [*glancing round*]: Why'd she go out? Was that Aunt Alice?

MEG: No. Aunt Alice is dead. She was run over.

HANNIBAL: Thought the face seemed familiar. Who was it then?

MEG [*pause*]: No one you know.

[BLACKOUT]

[INTERVAL]

Act Two

SCENE ONE

VILLAGERS *sing "The Helicopter Song," second verse, at front of stage while bar of the Spotted Pig is set up.*

VILLAGERS [*singing*]:

> Here comes the heli-
> Here comes the heli-
> Here comes the heli-
>   copter bringing us our post.
> A note for Mrs. Kelly,
> A box for Mr. Shelley,
> And a card for little Nelly
>   from her cousins on the coast.
> With *Guardian, Times* and Tele,
> Comics, Penguins, Peli-
>   Cans—and parcel for mine host.

CHORUS: No one in Street has to bother to shop, a
Housewife in Street can take her ease.
All she requires is delivered by chopper,
All of life's little necessities!
Life is a treat, living's so sweet
In Street!

[*Letters, etc., are distributed from basket as in Act One.
Then rope comes down with a large square carton covered
in red seals. It is deposited at side of stage.* VILLAGERS,
*opening and reading mail, take up positions at bar of
Spotted Pig. Narrow table at rear with white cloth over
it. Bottles, glasses, etc.* HANNAH, *looking pale and
wretched, serves drinks behind it. There are a couple of
small tables towards front of stage, and some bar stools.
As many* VILLAGERS *as possible.*

LILY *leads in* SUE, *dressed all in black with a white
apron, and solicitously seats her at one of the tables.*]

LILY [*exuding false sympathy*]: Just you sit down there,
dear, while I fetch you a drink. You'll be *much* better
here—where there's cheerful company—than moping
at home on your own. And a drink will do you good.

[*While she fetches* SUE's *drink, the* VILLAGERS *sing.*]

VILLAGERS [*singing; tune:* "Lillibullero"]:

Up with the pigs,
Down with the rats.
We'll clobber them all with
Cricket bats.
None of us wish
Ever to meet
The slobs on the o-
ther side of the street!

LILY [*returning with drinks for herself and* SUE, *sits
down*]: There you are, love. Now drink up. Just forget

about Meg Mirkin, and how rottenly she treated you. Honestly, it makes my blood boil whenever I think of it. She *is* the witch of Street, after all. She ought to have done *something* for Jenny.

SUE [*dully*]: I daresay she couldn't. They say since she got knocked down by a truck that she lost her power.

LILY [*sharp, interested*]: How does it work—the witch's power? You're Meg's sister-in-law—she must have talked to you about it?

SUE: Oh, yes, we used to talk a lot in the old days. When you could still get across the street. I was very fond of Meg then.

LILY: What happens—well, like, when the witch dies? How does she pass on her power?

SUE: Oh, it passes before that. When her eldest son marries—she hands over the wand and the ring to her son's wife. Or should.

LILY [*this is what she wanted to hear*]: Yes? Where does the power *come* from?

SUE [*surprised*]: Didn't your mother ever tell you all this?

LILY [*curtly*]: No. She was run over—when I was fifteen.

SUE: Oh—I see. Well, you know there was all Druids in the forest once—thousands of years ago?

LILY: In the forest? [*They both glance back uneasily.*] Yeah, I remember they said something about the Druids at school.

SUE: The Druids' power was all in two things—a sacred bull and a sacred serpent. Our teacher used to say that the king of the Druids *was* the sacred bull—he could change his shape when he chose. [*dreamily, after a pause*] They say—even now—the ghosts of the bulls sometimes come back at night and wander along the street.

LILY [*not interested*]: What about the ring?

SUE: Every year the sacred serpent laid an egg and died. The egg was a green stone.

LILY [*impatient*]: Yeah, yeah, so how did it get into the ring? How did the ring get into the village?

SUE: The story I heard was that after the Druids were all gone, a girl from the village found the green serpent's-egg stone in the forest. And had it made into a ring. And it gave her power. And she passed it on to her son's wife when she was old. And so it's been handed on ever since.

LILY: Definitely *her son's wife*, eh?

SUE: Her eldest son's wife.

LILY: So—if Meg Mirkin was to pass on the ring—it ought to be to Hannibal's wife?

SUE: If he's got one.

LILY [*starts to speak, checks herself*]: What about the sacred bull? Where did he come in?—Is there *still* one back there, in the forest? [*They both glance back again.*]

SUE: So I've heard. In my young days—when the wild bulls used to run through the street at the Bull Fair— the King Bull always led the herd. And the witch used to go out and touch him on the forehead—with the ring. And that brought good luck. But now the King Bull stays deep in the forest—I suppose he's angry. And Meg Mirkin's power has all dried up in her and turned her sick and old. [*slowly*] And there's no good luck anywhere. [*weeping*] And my Jenny's dead—oh, why did I get so angry with her? I can't bear to think of it. It was the traffic noise in my head. Even on her birthday I boxed her ears.

LILY [*false sympathy*]: Never mind, dear. Drink up.

SUE: I used to think, when she was a baby, that perhaps she'd marry Meg's Toomey—she was always fond of him—and then *she'd* have been witch of Street. [*weeping*]

LILY: I'll get you another drink. [*Stands up, takes* SUE's *glass, and walks towards bar. Pauses to mutter.*] Silly old bag! Her scrawny little Jenny wouldn't *ever* have been witch of Street.

VILLAGERS [*singing and laughing; tune:* "Streets of Laredo"]:

> Oh, the bull in the bush and the snake in the grass
> No longer can frighten and trample and sting.
> Who cares for them now as the trucks thunder past?
> Who cares for the power of an old magic ring?
>
> The snake in the grass and the bull in the bush
> No longer can plague us with fear or with grief.
> The serpent can't sting us, the bull cannot rush us,
> The snake is a belt—and the bull is roast beef!

LILY [*She puts* SUE's *drink on her table and stands looking darkly at the singers*]: Oh, those fools! Just let them wait till I get that ring on my finger again. Then they'll sing a different tune! [*fiercely, fists clenched*] Oh—I *wish* Hannibal Mirkin was here!

[*The square box delivered by helicopter begins to bump and agitate.*]

VILLAGER [*at bar, turning to look*]: Hey, Fred! Fred Steele! You'd better open your mail! I reckon there's mice in your parcel!

[FRED *comes in and undoes the cord. The box bursts open and* HANNIBAL *steps out. He bows.*]

VILLAGERS: Well, I never! Coo! Did you ever! What next! It's Hannibal Mirkin. What's *he* doing here? Why's he on this side? Get back to your own side of the street, etc., etc.

FRED [*quite cordial*]: Well, well, if it ain't Hannibal Mirkin! What brought you over the street?

HANNIBAL [*complacently*]: I gave the postman twenty nicker to drop me across.

VILLAGERS: A fool and his cash are soon parted. Who wants *him* here? Get back to your own rotten side. Boo!

HANNIBAL [*Strolling to bar. Jovial*]: Pretty smart, eh? Now I'm here, it's drinks all around! [*to* HANNAH] Hey, gorgeous, ladle them out! [*He plunks down a fistful of money on the bar.* HANNAH *looks nervously towards* FRED, *who nods.* LILY, *after a calculating glance at* HANNIBAL, *sits down again at lugubrious* SUE's *table.* SUE *is weeping, taking no notice of* HANNIBAL, *who, handing out drinks as* HANNAH *pours them, is soon the centre of a lively group.* FRED *walks over to* LILY.]

FRED [*quietly*]: Why aren't you helping with the customers?

LILY: Let Hannah look after them. I've done it plenty of times. [*looking daggers at* HANNIBAL] She can serve drinks to that rat.

FRED [*with quiet force*]: Now listen, my girl. I don't want any nonsense from you about Hannibal Mirkin being one of the Riverside lot. He brings in good money— *that's* what counts. Him going off and leaving you—

that's a long time back. Besides—who knows?—he might marry you still—now he's come back.

LILY [*enigmatically*]: Oh? You think he might marry me still—do you, Dad?

FRED: Why not? You never know! And he's a much better catch now, with a million quid in his knapsack. So you be civil to him, my girl.

LILY: Oh, yes. I'll be civil. I've got something to say to him. But it's *Hannah* he's interested in at the moment—not me. Look. [FRED *looks round, sees* HANNIBAL *giving* HANNAH *a big, ingratiating smile as he receives drink from her;* FRED *gets up and moves back to bar.*]

LILY [*between her teeth*]: So you'd like to pop a ring on little Hannah's finger now, would you, Hannibal Mirkin? Just you wait till I have *that* ring on my finger again. [*She sits watching him malevolently.*]

HANNIBAL [*to* HANNAH]: Fancy you growing up to be such a pretty girl! Little Hannah Steele! Mmmmm! You and me—Hannibal and Hannah! Sounds as if we was made for each other—doesn't it! How about you and me going to the pictures some evening, eh? Doesn't old Fred ever give you an evening off?

HANNAH [*terrified, glancing towards* LILY]: Oh, I couldn't! Besides, there *aren't* any pictures, except at Ebbchester, and you can't *get* there—except by helicopter.

HANNIBAL [*grandly*]: So—we'll go by helicopter. What if it does cost a hundred quid? *I'm* not mean!

HANNAH: No, thank you.

HANNIBAL: Oh, come on! Think of it! Up there in the blue—just you and me—and the pilot, of course. [*He *tries to put his arm round her. She evades him. He sings.*]

> When I take out my chick in the chopper
> The cherubs come chirping around
> For anything's perfectly proper
> When you're eighty feet up from the ground.

Come on now—say yes!

HANNAH [*distressed*]: Oh, thank you—but I'd much rather not.

HANNIBAL [*injured*]: *Why* not? I'm not cross-eyed!

FRED [*intervening sharply*]: Hannah! There's customers waiting for drinks. Hurry up and serve them.

HANNIBAL: That's right! Another round on me! Up the Forestsiders.

FRED [*leading* HANNIBAL *to small table and settling him*]: You and me's got to talk business, young man.

HANNIBAL: Sure! Whenever you want! Get us another drink first, though, Fred.

[FRED *takes glasses to bar. While* HANNIBAL *is sitting alone,* LILY *gets up and goes to him.*]

LILY [*with great intensity*]: Remember me?

HANNIBAL [*Looks at her vaguely, puzzled, then again. Doubtfully*]: Well—I—you're not Lily—*are* you?

LILY: That's right! Go to the top of the class. I'm Lily Steele.

HANNIBAL [*embarrassed*]: Well, well! Fancy meeting you again! Long time no see, et cetera. How—er—how are you getting on?

LILY: So you're planning to take Hannah to the pictures —are you? Isn't there a little something you've *forgotten*?

HANNIBAL: Eh? Forgotten?

LILY: A little matter between you and me?

HANNIBAL [*laughing indulgently, but wary*]: Oh, that's *long* ago! I'm not *quite* sure what you mean, but whatever it was, it's so long ago it doesn't count. Who cares what happened seventeen years back?

LILY: *I* care.

HANNIBAL [*laughing gaily*]: You can't be serious. Besides, you've got no proof. [*with more confidence*] You've got nothing in *writing*. [*exuberantly*] See? You've always gotta be sure you have things down on *paper*!

LILY: You think so, Hannibal Mirkin? [*He nods, beaming.*] You're wrong. You're so wrong! There's other kinds of proof. As you will soon find out.

[*She goes out as* FRED *returns with drinks.*]

FRED [*sitting down*]: Now, listen here. This is why I wrote to you. Cheers.

HANNIBAL: Cheers.

FRED: This village has gone to the dogs. As you can see. What we need is a bypass. Then Street would be a decent little place—like it was once. We'd get tourists stopping for meals as they used to. Trade would pick up.

HANNIBAL: Yeah, I was thinking of starting one of my bars here, but what would be the use, the way it is now? It's horrible.

FRED: Well, whose fault's that?

HANNIBAL [*impatient*]: No use blaming *me*. It would have happened anyway. So let them put in a bypass. What's stopping them?

FRED: Nowhere to put it. River your side of the street—forest on ours.

HANNIBAL: Why can't they run a road through the forest?

[*They both glance over their shoulders.*]

FRED: It's too dangerous. Wild white bulls. Ghosts of the old Druids from way back. Old King Cunobel—used to be head Druid in the year minus two thousand—they say *he's* still around in the shape of a giant white bull. Anyone goes through that forest with hate in his heart—King Cunobel gets him. Well—that's not a healthy locality for a dual highway!

HANNIBAL: Wouldn't worry me. [*complacently*] I've got no hate in my heart.

FRED: Wouldn't do for the people in *this* town. The Riverside lot hate us—and we can't stick *them*.

HANNIBAL: If the forest's no go—where can you put the bypass?

FRED: It's simple. [*He unrolls a plan.*] I've a pal on the County Council who says he can swing it for fifty thousand. Right?

HANNIBAL: So far, so good.

FRED: All we have to do is knock down all the houses on the riverbank side of the street. Put the bypass there. See?

HANNIBAL [*wary*]: What about the people in them?

FRED: There aren't as many as there were. [*grinning*] I've had trucks accidentally knock into quite a few. And their houses. And I've bought up others, quietlike. There's your mum, of course. Could you persuade her to move?

HANNIBAL: I don't think she'd be keen—

FRED: Suppose you built her a nice little bungalow—out by Potash Crossing? I've some land out there.

HANNIBAL: I think she'd be hard to shift.

FRED: Maybe it would be kinder to put her in a nursing home? My sister runs a home for old folks in Coalbury. After all, your mother's getting on now. And she's crippled. Then we can get out the other people—once she's gone.

HANNIBAL: Yeah, I see—and then you run your road through.

FRED: There'd be space in front of the old Pig for a car park—and a tea garden—you could have your Burger Bar at the other end of the village—or we could go into partnership.

HANNIBAL: Everyone's happy!

FRED [*enthusiastic*]: Right. Hannah! Bring us another glass of wine. All we need [*looking hopefully at* HANNIBAL] is fifty thousand.

HANNIBAL: Well—that might be managed. Listen— suppose I were to marry your daughter—the *younger* one, I mean—I wouldn't mind handing over fifty thousand.

[HANNAH *brings glasses of wine to their table. As she does so,* HANNIBAL *pinches her cheek. She flinches away, and he gives her plait quite a sharp tug.*]

FRED: Yes—I see. [*as* HANNAH *is about to go*] Wait a minute, Hannah my dear. Listen to this. Here's Mr. Mirkin wants to marry you. Been all round the world, rolling in money, come back to Street, and he wants to marry *you*. Aren't you a lucky girl? [*giving her a mean-*

ing look] So you better say yes, *thank* you, to him. Nicely, now!

HANNAH: But I don't want to marry him! Not at all!

FRED [*indignant*]: Are you out of your *mind*? Here I've fed and reared and looked after you all these years and is this the reward I get? You'll do as you're told, my girl! You'll marry him and like it! Say yes—*now*—at *once*! Say yes, thank you, Mr. Mirkin!

HANNAH: No! I won't!

HANNIBAL [*a bit crestfallen*]: Oh, come on, ducks! Be reasonable! What's the matter with me?

FRED: I'm warning you, girl! You'd better say yes! Or you might have to be shut up in a barrel again. And it would be for longer this time. *Much* longer. [*grasping her wrist*] Well? Is it yes?

[LILY, *who has come back, stands watching with fierce attention.* HANNAH *picks up a glass of wine and throws it in* HANNIBAL's *face.*]

HANNAH: You spoilt our village. You caused dozens of deaths. *That's* what I think of you!

FRED [*outraged*]: Lily—lock her in her bedroom. I'll deal with her later. You'll soon find out what it means to cross me, my girl!

[LILY *starts to drag* HANNAH *away. She is much stronger.*]

[BLACKOUT]

SCENE TWO

Two groups of VILLAGERS *shouting across front of stage at each other while street scene is established.*

FIRST GROUP [*shouting*]:

> We—hate—you—Riverside hicks.
> We'll clobber you all with hockey sticks.

SECOND GROUP [*shouting*]:

> We—hate—you—Forestside swine.
> We'd like to drown you in turpentine.

[*They go out. The street is seen at night. Street lamps lit. Sound of traffic dies and is replaced by bellowing and sound of hoofs. Shadows of* BULLS *pass across houses.*

HANNAH *and* TOOMEY *appear on balconies.*]

HANNAH [*singing last two verses of their song and signaling*]:

> I love you through the hours of dark, I love you through
>   the day,
> But attend to what I say:
> There's danger in delay!
> I think they'll even kill me if I don't do what they say.
> They'll kill me if I don't do what they say!

TOOMEY [*singing and signaling*]:

> The best laid schemes of mice and men quite often gang
>   a-gley,
> So attend to what I say:
> You'll *have* to disobey!
> Why don't we get together and arrange to run away?
> Why don't we just arrange to run away?

VILLAGERS [*who have gathered in street while singing was going on*]: Traitors! Lynch them! Throw them in the river! Dump them in the forest!

[FRED *and* LILY *appear behind* HANNAH.]

FRED: Right! That settles it! Since you can't be trusted in your room, it's back to the barrel for you, my girl. Down in the cellar.

[HANNAH *waves despairingly to* TOOMEY *as she is dragged away*.]

TOOMEY [*comes down from balcony and calls up from street*]: Hannah!

[VILLAGERS *chase him and he runs to and fro, avoiding them. While this is going on, the Mirkin house frame is reversed and the Mirkin kitchen set up*.]

[BLACKOUT]

SCENE THREE

The Mirkin kitchen. MEG *in her wheelchair.* HANNIBAL'*s bicycle leaning against wall.* TOOMEY *runs in, excited and distressed.*

TOOMEY [*glancing round cautiously*]: Where's Hannibal?

MEG: He paid the postman twenty pounds to take him over to the Spotted Pig.

TOOMEY: Mother! They're going to make Hannah *marry* him—her father says she's got to! I can't *stand* it!

MEG: How do you know that?

TOOMEY: She told me—in our sign language. Now her father's locked her in the cellar. She's shut up inside a *barrel*! I'll *have* to get her away *somehow*. *Please* help us. Can't you?

[*With difficulty, because of his stiff leg, he kneels in front of her chair and takes her hand. The ring flashes.*]

MEG: Sometimes you look just like your father.

TOOMEY: Can't you help us, Mother?

MEG: Yes—the way things are—I think I must. It will be only human help, though. No magic about it. And it will be dangerous.

TOOMEY: Never mind that.

MEG [*glancing round*]: Quick, then—before Hannibal gets back. Look in the table drawer. You'll find a forked stick.

[*He opens drawer, finds stick.*]

MEG: Good. Now—take it in your hands, thumbs pointing back—like this [*she demonstrates*]; now, holding it, walk to and fro, all over the room.

TOOMEY [*doing so*]: Why? I don't understand. What's the point?

MEG: You'll see, I hope. Go on. [*He limps to and fro.*] Don't miss any part of the floor. [*musingly*] When Lily Steele snatched the serpent's-egg ring from me the other day, I suddenly understood *why* it hasn't worked for me for so long. It wasn't because my legs were broken by the truck. That had nothing to do with it. [*She is almost talking to herself.*] No—it's because Lily is the real witch. The serpent's egg knows its true owner. It is angry. I can feel it all the time—burning and pulling —it wants to get off my finger. [*She holds up her hand, staring at it.*] Just for those few minutes, yesterday, when I wasn't wearing it, I felt so light and free— happier than I have since your father died.

TOOMEY [*still limping to and fro*]: *Lily* its owner? [*amazed*] But—how can she be?

MEG: She and your brother must have been married secretly before he went off.

TOOMEY [*wonderingly, pausing*]: Lily and Hannibal *married*? You really think so?

MEG: Yes. I'm sure of it.

TOOMEY: But why wouldn't she have told her father?

MEG: After Hannibal had gone off—and become so unpopular? You know what Fred Steele's like. He'd have been terribly angry. It's different now Hannibal's rich.

TOOMEY: But if Hannibal's married to Lily—then he can't marry Hannah.

MEG: He's not to be trusted, I'm afraid. He might tell some lie—if Lily has no proof.

TOOMEY [*perturbed*]: But if Lily's the ring's real owner —oughtn't she to *have* it?

MEG: She's so full of hate. I'm afraid of what she might do with it.

TOOMEY: But if you *gave* it to her—she might feel better?

MEG: Oh—I'm not sure, I'm not sure! [*distressed, rubbing her forehead*] I'm not sure what's the right thing to do. Why won't the ring *tell* me? If Lily had it— she might do terrible harm to everyone in Street. There's a lot of power in the ring. If I only knew what it wanted.

TOOMEY: Oh! Look! [*The stick in his hands has swung down and points, quivering, to a spot on the floor.*]

MEG: Ah! That's what I hoped. Get your saw, Toomey, and cut a hole there, big enough to climb through. Big enough to lower a bicycle through. Hurry!

[*He gets a saw and proceeds to cut a square traphole in the floor while she talks.*]

MEG: If you take Hannah away—you realize you won't be able to come back?

TOOMEY [*He sits back and gapes at her, horrified.*]: Not come back? *Ever?*

MEG: How do you think the two of you could manage, married to each other, in Street? Which side of the street would you live on?

TOOMEY [*in anguish*]: But—we were *born* here. It's our home.

MEG: You've got to see this, Toomey. The way things are, you and Hannah can't come back. Everybody would hate you.

TOOMEY: But—

MEG: Don't stop. Go on sawing. If Hannibal were to come in now—

TOOMEY: But who's going to look after *you*? *He* won't.

MEG: It doesn't matter about me.

TOOMEY: But we can't just go off and leave you. They'd —they might—I don't like to think what they might do to you.

MEG [*looks searchingly at him*]: How brave are you, Toomey?

TOOMEY: I don't know.

MEG: You and Hannah really love one another?

TOOMEY: Oh, *yes.*

MEG [*after a pause*]: When your cousin Jenny was dying —what did she tell you?

TOOMEY: It—it was private.

MEG: I see: [*musingly*] She told you that she loved you. [*She looks at him. He is silent.*] Poor Jenny. I'm glad she was able to tell you. That was a big gift she gave you. And it may help you. Things like that aren't wasted.

TOOMEY: I don't understand.

MEG: When you and Hannah leave—I know now what you must do. You must go into the forest.

TOOMEY: The forest? But nobody goes there! What about the bulls?

MEG: Pay no attention to them. Go calmly past. Don't fear them. Think about each other.

TOOMEY: They aren't savage?

MEG: They won't be if you are quiet. Your father and I were in the forest once—we saw the bulls—they didn't attack us.

TOOMEY: Did you see the King Bull? [*awestruck*] King Cunobel's ghost?

MEG: What we saw then is not important now. Listen, this is not just for you—it's for the whole village. You have to find King Cunobel's grave.

TOOMEY: Yes—why?

MEG: It's a long way. Miles in. Right in the middle. That's why you'll need the bicycle.

TOOMEY: How shall we know the grave?

MEG: There's a huge thicket. And a great oak stump with Cunobel's name carved on it. When you get there, you must call him.

TOOMEY [*nervous*]: *Call* him? How?

MEG: Just call. And when he comes—give him a gift.

TOOMEY: Aha! [*He has sawed right round. He lifts out square of wood.*] Oh! [*looking down into hole*] Why— there's *water* down below! I never knew! It's absolutely rushing past.

MEG [*calmly*]: Yes. It's the brook from the forest, that

runs into the river. If you get into it and go upstream
—you'll have to drag the bicycle or push it.

TOOMEY: *I* see! We can get into the forest. It must
go right under the street. [*troubled*] But what about
Hannah?

MEG: The stream runs under the street and through the
cellar of the Spotted Pig. [*dryly*] Your father always
used to say Fred Steele put water in the beer.

TOOMEY: Oh, that's great. I can get out into the cellar
and find Hannah—let her out.

MEG: But mind! When the stream is full, after rain, it
sometimes fills the tunnel right up. You may have to
go under water for part of the way—can you do that?

TOOMEY [*nervous but resolute*]: I'll just have to.

MEG: Can you hold your breath while you count fifty—
slowly?

TOOMEY: I'll try. [*He does so, counting by wagging a
finger up and down. While he does this,* MEG *slowly
takes off her green ring, looks at it as if for a last con-
sultation, presses it to her forehead, and kisses it good-
bye.*]

TOOMEY [*letting out his breath with a gasp*]: Fifty! Did
it!

MEG: I hope Hannah can too.

TOOMEY [*up against a problem*]: Mother? You said we
have to call—K—King Cunobel and give him a gift.
What is he? Is he a man or a bull?

MEG: He might be either.

TOOMEY: And what gift can we give him?

MEG: This. [*She holds out her ring.*]

TOOMEY: The serpent's egg. [*awestruck*] What will he do with it?

MEG: I think he has been wanting it for a long time. Ever since it was lost. I hope—I believe—that when he has it again—it will be better for everyone. Maybe it will produce some *change*.

TOOMEY: In him? Or us? What kind of change?

MEG: I don't know. Like—the change from winter to summer. You can hardly *believe* it. But it happens. If only we could *step aside*—

TOOMEY [*mystified*]: Out of the street, you mean?

MEG [*half smiling*]: Perhaps! Out of the narrow track we are stuck in. Time is just a line—if we could leave it—

[*Sound of steps.*]

MEG: Quick, here's Hannibal!

[TOOMEY *has tied cord to bicycle. He lowers it through the hole.*]

MEG: Put on the ring. It will help you make your way upstream. It has that power.

TOOMEY [*suddenly irresolute, terribly worried*]: You're sure you'll be all right?

MEG: Yes—yes—go!

TOOMEY [*holding end of cord*]: We'll come back— somehow, we'll come back.

[*He kisses her, takes a huge breath, and climbs into the hole, pulling the square of wood back after him. It falls slightly askew.* MEG, *moving her wheelchair, is able to mask it from* HANNIBAL, *who comes in looking rather disgruntled. While they talk, she reaches down with the forked stick and pushes the square into place.*]

HANNIBAL: What was that noise?

MEG: Probably something falling off a shelf upstairs.

[*She takes a deep breath, as if timing* TOOMEY, *and is seen to be counting, nodding her head slightly.*]

HANNIBAL [*looks at her, frowning*]: Are you all right? [*She nods.*] Well, you don't look it! Listen—I've been thinking you don't seem at all well. I think you ought to go away for a bit right away from here. For a change.

[MEG *looks at him inquiringly but can't speak; she is still counting.*]

HANNIBAL: There's a nice little nursing home I know of only fifty miles from here—first-rate medical care, their own vegetables, fully trained staff—how'd you like a few weeks in there—eh?

MEG [*letting out her breath with a gasp*]: Forty-nine— fifty—no, thank you, Hannibal. It's a kind thought, but I'm better at home. I don't want to leave Street.

HANNIBAL [*annoyed*]: Now—doesn't that just *show*! You're in such bad shape that you don't even *want* a change.

MEG: Oh, yes—I want a change.

HANNIBAL [*taking her hand*]: Look at you—all out of breath—your pulse is going pit-a-pat and you're quite white. What the devil's this? [*taking the forked stick from her*] Looks like a catapult with no elastic.

MEG [*laughing with a touch of hysteria*]: That's right—a catapult. Put a bit of elastic in it and we could shoot peas at the Forestsiders.

HANNIBAL [*puzzled, suspicious*]: You really *are* ill—I believe you're feverish. I'm going to phone Fred Steele right away and get him to fix up a place at that home. [*he starts out, then turns to say*] Where's Toomey? I want a word with him.

MEG: I sent him on an errand.

[BLACKOUT]

SCENE FOUR

VILLAGERS *enter singing "The Street Song," third verse.*
VILLAGERS:

> If life is your favourite habit,
> And death is not your treat,
> Look to the right, look to the left,
> Look to the right again, look to the left again—
> *And then: don't cross the street!*

While they sing front stage, the cellar of the Spotted Pig is set up. Drapes painted with bricks hung over frames, a couple of barrels, a candle in a bottle, wine racks, one or two cases of bottles. Suggestion of water at rear, light-reflections moving on backdrop. No traffic sound, but possibly water dripping.

HANNAH [*inside barrel, calling loudly*]: Help—help! Let me out! Father—Lily—don't leave me in here! Somebody—let me out! Toomey—I'm in here!

[LILY *comes in to pick up a case of bottles. Pauses by barrel.*]

LILY [*lifting barrel lid*]: No use calling to *me*. Father says you've got to stay in there till you agree to marry Hannibal.

HANNAH: Oh, Lily—please let me out!

LILY: Not likely! *I* don't want you marrying Hannibal. You can stay in there till you starve, for all I care.

HANNAH: I'll *never* marry Hannibal.

LILY: No. You're right there. [*going out*] Wish *I* could stop in a barrel. There's about a million customers in the bar—and Sue Thatcher snoring away as if she was in church. [*Goes out.*]

HANNAH [*kicks inside of barrel*]: Toomey—Toomey— I'm in here! Oh, I wish you'd come! You did say you'd try to! [*pause*] Toomey! Toomey!

[*After a moment or two* SUE *comes in. She looks bewildered, as if just woken from sleep.*]

SUE: Who's that calling? Thought I heard Jenny's voice calling me. All right, love, Mommy's coming. Are you thirsty? Did you want a drink of water? Jenny?

[*She rubs her eyes, shakes her head, looks round dazedly.*]

SUE: What ever am I doing down *here*? I believe this is Fred Steele's cellar. I must have been dreaming— thought I heard Jenny's voice.

HANNAH: Help! Help! Let me out!

SUE [*startled to death*]: Is there somebody in there?

HANNAH: Help! It's Hannah! I'm in here!

[SUE *lifts off lid and looks in.*]

SUE: Why—it *is* Hannah! Oh, you poor little thing! Did Fred and Lily put you in there? Oh, that was cruel. Wait—I'll soon help you out. Oh, I do call that a shame.

[*She helps out* HANNAH, *whose hands have been tied behind her; unties her hands.*]

HANNAH: Oh—*thank you*, Mrs. Thatcher.

SUE: But why did they put you *in* there—I don't understand.

HANNAH: Because I love Toomey Mirkin—I want to marry him.

SUE: You want to marry Toomey Mirkin? [*sadly*] My Jenny did, too. She didn't think I knew it, but I did. She loved him.

HANNAH: Jenny loved him? [SUE *nods.*] Oh, *poor* Jenny. [HANNAH *looks rather hopelessly round the cellar, then clasps* SUE'*s hands.*] Mrs. Thatcher! Please will you help me—for Jenny's sake—will you help me to get out of here?

SUE: For Jenny's sake. [*slowly*] Yes—all right. What do you want me to do?

HANNAH: If I could go to your house—if you could talk to Father and Lily—distract their attention—I could slip out the back way—climb over the fence into your garden.

SUE: You could hide in my house.

HANNAH: I could signal to Toomey from your window.

SUE: Quick, then, let's go now. There's quite a few people in the bar; they're busy.

HANNAH: Wait—I must leave a message for Toomey in case he comes here—he promised he'd try to help me. What can I write on?

SUE: Here, my apron—there's a pencil in the pocket.

[*She takes off her apron.* HANNAH *writes on it.*]

HANNAH [*writing*]: Toomey—Jenny's mother knows where I am.

[*She ties apron strings round top of barrel, so that the*

*apron is towards the audience and away from the entrance
used by* FRED *and* LILY.]

HANNAH: There—let's hope they don't notice it.

SUE: Hurry up—let's go—don't make a sound. [*They
tiptoe out.*]

[*After a short pause,* FRED *comes in with crate of empties.
He stops by barrel and speaks.*]

FRED: Hannah? Are you listening? [*pause*] Not quite so
perky in there now, eh? Well—I can tell you—you're
going to have plenty of time to think. Because you're
not coming out of that barrel till you promise to marry
Hannibal Mirkin.

LILY [*Just putting her head onstage. She sounds annoyed*]:
Father? Are you there? Phone for you—you're wanted
on the telephone by Mr. Hannibal Mirkin. He wishes to
speak to you about a nursing home.

FRED: All right, I'm coming. [*He picks up case and goes
out.*]

LILY [*coming farther in*]: Funny, I thought I saw Sue
Thatcher wandering towards the cellar stair, half asleep.
Guess she woke up and wandered off home. Good rid-
dance, the old misery.

[*Picking up bottles, she sees the apron on the barrel. She
darts across, reads the message, lifts the lid, looks in
barrel.*]

LILY: Well—I'll—be—! Sue Thatcher! Just wait till I
tell her what I think of her, the old nosy parker. [*She
moves as if to pursue them, then stops.*] Hmmm! So
we're expecting young Master Toomey Mirkin, are we?
Fancy that now! Seeing quite a little bit of the Mirkin
family lately. Well, young Master Toomey is in for a
big surprise when he arrives.

VOICES OF CUSTOMERS [*shouting*]: Hurry up with those drinks, Lily—we're thirsty!

LILY: Just a minute! I shan't be long—ask Father to look after you.

[TOOMEY *arrives from backstage, wheeling the bike, which he leans against a barrel. His hair is wet, and he is exhausted and panting.*]

TOOMEY [*calling softly*]: Hannah? Hannah? Are you there? Hannah?

[LILY *is galvanized at the sound of his voice and slips behind a barrel, holding a bottle.* TOOMEY *begins searching about. Sees* SUE's *apron, and kneels down to read its message with a torch. As he is doing so,* LILY *steals up behind him and bangs him on the head with the bottle. He falls senseless.*]

LILY [*with huge satisfaction*]: That'll teach *you* to come crawling into our cellar—you little worm! [*She sees the ring on his outstretched hand.*] Oh! My ring! [*astonished*] My ring! [*gloating*] Now I've got that crooked—swindling—thieving—lying—*skunk* in my power. *Now* I've got him where I want him!

[*She puts on the ring, admiring its flash in the light of the candle in the bottle, which she holds in her other hand. Then stands in declamatory position, hand with ring upraised.*]

LILY: I curse Hannibal Mirkin! Curse him—curse him—curse him—*curse him*! I curse him for all the harm he did me—for marrying me and then going off and leaving me—for seventeen wasted years of my life—for my mother, killed by a truck—for my brother, killed by a truck—curse him, curse him, curse him, curse him!

[*Overcome by the power of the curse, she shudders and*

slowly sinks to huddled position on the floor as TOOMEY
begins to stir.]

[BLACKOUT]

SCENE FIVE

Front stage, with backdrop as at beginning of Act One.
SUE *and* HANNAH *slip in, looking warily about.*

SUE [*horrified*]: Oh, my Lord!

HANNAH: What's the matter?

SUE: My front-door key! I forgot it!

HANNAH: Where is it?

SUE: It's in my apron pocket—in the cellar!

HANNAH: I'll go back for it.

SUE: No, you will not! *I'll* go. They can't do anything to
me. You wait in my garden till I come back. If they
come for you—if there's trouble—slip into the forest.

[*They go out different ways. After a moment* HANNIBAL
comes in with a VILLAGER.]

HANNIBAL [*complacently*]: Just fixed for my poor old
mother to go into a nursing home. It's much the best
thing for her—she really can't look after herself any
more.

VILLAGER: That's right—best thing you can do for 'em.
[*he stares past* HANNIBAL *and exclaims*] Why, there's
Lily Steele—what ever is she doing, holding that candle
as if she were sleepwalking? She's going right into the
middle of the *street*—is she crazy or something?

[LILY, *exactly as in previous scene, carrying candle in
bottle, walks to midstage and stands as before.*]

LILY: I curse Hannibal Mirkin! Curse him—curse him—curse him—*curse him*! I curse him for all the harm he did me—for marrying me and then going off and leaving me—for seventeen wasted years of my life—for my mother, killed by a truck—for my brother, killed by a truck—curse him, curse him, curse him, curse him! [*She slowly moves offstage.*]

HANNIBAL [*injured*]: Here, what are you going on like that for? What's she going on like that for? What did I do that was so wrong? Nothing different from lots of others! Spiteful cow! Just because she's lost her looks and I prefer her sister. As for getting married, that's all a load of cod—she's raving! Hey—that's queer—there's *Father*! Right out there in the middle of the traffic. Hey —*Dad*! Come off the road, you'll get hurt, you'll get killed! Oh, my Gawd—[*watching in horror as his father does invisibly get killed*]—*right* under a blooming truck! Mind that dog—you little *fool*! Mary! Come back! Chico! Come here! Cripes, there's Mother—*Mother*! Don't try to cross carrying Toomey—he's too heavy for you—come back!

[*He is moving from side to side, sometimes starting forward, then hesitating and drawing back as if invisible trucks whizzed past him.*]

HANNIBAL: Oh, Gawd! It's gone right over them. Stop it—*stop* it! Mrs. Steele—Mr. Baker—come back!

[*Appalled, seeing all the accidents that have happened in Street for the past seventeen years, he rushes into the middle of the stage, trying to save invisible people, stop invisible traffic. There is a terrific screech of brakes, and he falls under the wheels of an invisible truck.*]

VILLAGERS [*appearing in two groups at sides of stage*]:

What got *into* him? Seems like he went off his head! Well, he's done for, that's certain. Right under a truck. Terrible, terrible. Hardly a day passes but there's another . . . he'd only just come home, too. Hush, there's his mother. . . .

[MEG *appears in her wheelchair at side of stage.* FRED *comes out on the other side. They stare at one another over* HANNIBAL'*s body as lights dim. Tune of "The Street Song" played mournfully.*]

[BLACKOUT]

SCENE SIX

The Spotted Pig cellar as before. LILY *and* TOOMEY *are in the same positions.* TOOMEY *pulls himself up, totters over, and gazes wonderingly at* LILY. *Then, seeing the ring on her hand, takes it off and puts it on his own finger.*

SUE *tiptoes in, sees* TOOMEY, *and gasps.*

SUE: Oh, my heart! Toomey—is that you? What ever has happened to Lily?

TOOMEY [*bewildered*]: I don't know. I think she must have hit me with a bottle—but now she seems to have fainted.

SUE: Well—quick—don't you wait here! Hannah's waiting for you in my garden. Hurry up and slip out the back way! Fred Steele won't see you if you go fast; everyone's out front. Something [*she looks at him, remembers* HANNIBAL *is his brother*]—something bad has happened in the street.

[TOOMEY *nods, starts out.*]

SUE [*calling softly after him*]: You can stop in my house if you like—here's the key.

TOOMEY: Thanks, Mrs. Thatcher—thank you very much —but we won't stay. We're going into the forest.

SUE: The *forest*—what for—[LILY *stirs*] *quick*, she's coming to.

LILY [*dazedly, pulling herself up*]: What happened? Everything went all hot and red—I felt as if I was breathing smoke—I—it seemed as if I was in the street. Hannibal was there. [*She sees* SUE.] Sue Thatcher? [*angrily*] If you think you can come into our cellar and let out Hannah, you're mistaken—oh! [*Standing up, she sees empty barrel and remembers.*] Where's Toomey Mirkin?

SUE [*calmly*]: He's gone, Lily.

LILY: Gone to *your* house? With Hannah? I'll soon fetch them back! How *dare* you interfere—how dare you come poking into our affairs?

SUE: No. They aren't at my house.

LILY: Where, then?

SUE: Where you won't catch them. In the forest.

LILY: The *forest*? Oh, won't I? First I'll deal with you— oh! [*For the first time she notices that the ring is gone again.*] *Who* took my ring? Have you got it—you—

[*She advances menacingly on* SUE, *who steps back.*]

SUE: I've got no ring of yours.

LILY [*gathering rage*]: That little rat Toomey must have snatched it—*he*'ll be sorry when I catch up with him. I'll deal with him the way I did with his brother—I'll burn him—I'll wither him up—I'll soon catch them!

[*Sees bike and wheels it out.*]

[SUE *unties her apron from the barrel and is about to leave when* FRED *comes in.*]

FRED: What the devil's going on down here? Where's Lily? Someone said she'd been seen in the street— shouting at Hannibal—saying she was his wife. I thought she was down here.

SUE: Yes, she was. She's just gone off. Said she was going into the forest.

FRED: Why'd she do that? [*lower voice*] Did she know Hannibal was dead?

SUE: I don't know. She was going on about a ring. Fred —I think she *killed* Hannibal Mirkin.

FRED: *Killed* him? How *could* she? If she was down here.

SUE: I think she was his wife.

FRED: His *wife*? How could she be? In that case— [*He ponders.*] His wife? But in that case—she stands to inherit a million.

[*He does not look as cheerful as might be expected—in fact he looks blank.* SUE *ties her apron round her waist, reassures herself that the key is in the pocket, and walks out.*]

[BLACKOUT]

SCENE SEVEN

The forest. This should be as magic and mysterious as possible, with swags of grey gauze dangling; house frames, wrapped in the same material, could be thickets. Among them, motionless, the figures of seven huge white BULLS. *While scene is set up,* VILLAGERS, *dressed in black hats and black capes, sing "Forest Song."*

VILLAGERS [*singing softly*]:

> Listen to the forest
> Listen to its voices
> Listen to the whisper
> Of leaves and stems and grasses
> Listen to the whisper
> Listen: understand,
> Nothing here can hurt you
> The forest is your friend.

> CHORUS: Green—breathing—silent—calm
> Hold here—no thought of harm
> Wise wood—proud trees
> Love here—lives at ease.

[TOOMEY *and* HANNAH *tiptoe in. They look tired and draggled.* TOOMEY *is limping badly.*]

TOOMEY: I should think we're safe here for a little. Are you tired? Shall we have a rest?

HANNAH: Oh, yes! [*They sit down wearily.*] We must have come miles and miles.

TOOMEY: Isn't it quiet—you'd think we were hundreds of miles from *anywhere.*

HANNAH [*dreamily*]: Perhaps we are. Perhaps we really *have* come hundreds of miles. It's like a different world.

TOOMEY: You'd never think the street went past it. Perhaps that's what Mother meant by stepping aside.

HANNAH: Oh! [*Suddenly noticing* BULLS *among trees. She grabs his arm.*]

TOOMEY [*looking at his foot*]: I must have grazed my foot on a rock. It keeps bleeding.

HANNAH: Toomey—look at the bulls! [*She is trembling.*]

TOOMEY [*moving close to her, puts protective arm round her shoulders*]: Hush! They won't hurt you. Don't be frightened.

HANNAH: They're so *huge*. Are you sure they won't hurt us?

TOOMEY: Not if we don't annoy them. Or touch one of their calves.

HANNAH: What would happen then?

TOOMEY: First they'd kill the calf.

HANNAH: Their own calf?

TOOMEY: They won't let themselves be touched. Ever.

HANNAH: And then—what would they do?

TOOMEY: Then they'd kill us. They'd get into a semi-circle—all their horns touching. If you see them do that—you know you have to run for your life—climb a tree.

HANNAH: Just the same, they're very beautiful.—How do you know all this?

TOOMEY: I'm not sure. I just remember it.

HANNAH: Toomey?

TOOMEY: What? What is it?

HANNAH: It's so queer—this is the first time we've talked to each other. We're talking in *words*—instead of our sign language!

TOOMEY [*simply*]: I feel as if I'd been with you always.

HANNAH: Just the same—I rather miss our sign language.

[*She sketches a few signs; he does too.*]

BOTH [*singing last two verses of "Jenny's Song"*]:

> I love *you*.
> *You* love *me*.
> Oh, how blessed by
> Luck are we.

> You love me.
> I love you.
> There is nothing
> Else to do.

HANNAH: That's queer.

TOOMEY: What is it?

HANNAH: Just for a moment—I thought I saw your cousin Jenny sitting by us.

[*Rested, they get up and slowly walk out.*]

[BLACKOUT]

SCENE EIGHT

Same scene. LILY *comes in, riding or pushing bike.*

LILY [*loud, threatening voice*]: Toomey! Hannah! I can see you—you might as well come out. I'm going to catch you. I've been following your tracks all along. Aha! [*She spots the place where they were sitting.*] There's a bit of blood on the ground. It's wet—that proves they were here only a minute ago. Toomey! Hannah! I'm going to catch you. I want my ring!

[*She rings the bicycle bell, loudly and persistently. She is about to get back on the bike when she looks up and sees that seven great* BULLS *have come out from the trees and*

*are slowly converging on her in a semicircle. She gives a
shriek.*]

LILY: *Oh! Help! Help!* Toomey—Hannah—come and
help me!

[*At first she runs to and fro but is trapped by the converging* BULLS. *At last she gives in and drops to her knees,
head and arms bowed forward. In silence they cluster
round her. Lights dim. Then there is a tremendous noise
of bellowing.*]

[BLACKOUT]

SCENE NINE

Same scene. BULLS *and* LILY *are gone. In their place is a
tree stump.* HANNAH *and* TOOMEY *come in.*

TOOMEY: I think this is it. Mother said the very thickest
part of the forest.

HANNAH [*awestruck*]: It's certainly very dark here.

TOOMEY: Look—there's the stump—the king's grave—
it should have his name carved.

[*They feel about on top of the stump.*]

HANNAH: Yes—I can feel letters—they're almost covered with moss—but I can feel them. What do we do
now?

TOOMEY: We have to call him.

HANNAH [*nervously*]: How do we do that?

TOOMEY [*cupping his hands round his mouth and calling
softly*]: Lord of the Bulls! Hear us calling and come to
our aid!

HANNAH: Lord of the Bulls! Come to us here by the king's grave.

TOOMEY: Come to us!

HANNAH: Come to us!

[*Soft sound of drumming hoofs is heard.*]

TOOMEY [*anxious for* HANNAH]: Do you want to climb up a tree? I think he's coming!

HANNAH [*suddenly collected*]: No. I know what to do. Give me the ring! [*She calls.*] Lord of the Bulls! Hear what we have brought you: the serpent's egg, the sacred apple, thrown from the nest of serpents, caught in the white apron, grafted in the ring! Gift of shrewd speaking, strength to float against the current, valor in combat. We have brought it back! [*She takes the ring from* TOOMEY.]

[*The sound of hoofs becomes louder and louder. A large white* BULL *comes in, head lowered menacingly.* HANNAH *walks towards it, touches it on the forehead with the ring, then hangs the ring on one of its horns. The* BULL, *standing midstage, becomes bathed in light and shines; snorts, paws the ground, and looks round proudly. Tremendous bellow is heard. Then it paces majestically out.* TOOMEY *and* HANNAH, *hand in hand, watch it out of sight.*]

[BLACKOUT]

SCENE TEN

VILLAGERS *enter singing last verse of "The Street Song." They carry capes, wear matadors' hats as at start of Act One.*

VILLAGERS [*singing*]:

> If you want to live in a healthy spot
> That's off the normal beat
> Don't go to France, don't go to Spain
> Don't go to Florida, don't go to Mexico—
> But just: come down to Street!

> CHORUS: Life is sweet in Street,
>   Life is sweet in Street!
>   Live to a hundred on your old-age pension,
>   Come along and live in Street.

While they sing front stage, the street scene is set up. There are flowers in small plots in front of houses. Creepers on house fronts. Small tables in front of the Spotted Pig. Bird song is heard, possibly cuckoo calling. VILLAGERS *stroll to and fro, chatting.*

TOOMEY *and* HANNAH *walk in hand in hand.* TOOMEY *no longer limps. They look round in astonishment.*

HANNAH: Look at the flowers! Where did they come from?

TOOMEY: There's grass growing—even in the street!

HANNAH: It's so quiet—where's all the traffic?

TOOMEY: Oh, look—there's Mother.

[FRED *comes in pushing* MEG *in her wheelchair.* SUE *walks beside. They are having a quiet, pleasant conversation.*]

TOOMEY: Mother!

HANNAH: Father!

MEG [*placidly*]: Why, it's the children. Isn't that nice? Just in time for tea. Would you like to put the kettle on, Fred?

FRED: All right, my dear. Shall we have tea outside?

MEG: Yes—why not? It's a lovely warm afternoon.

FRED [*gives* HANNAH *a kiss, as* TOOMEY *goes to hug* MEG]: You've grown as pretty as a picture, dearie. [*Shakes* TOOMEY's *hand.*] Glad to have you back, my boy. [*He goes out.*]

TOOMEY [*bewildered*]: I don't understand! What happened? Where's all the traffic?

MEG: We stepped aside. Do you remember what I was saying?

TOOMEY: Yes, but—how do you mean, stepped aside?

MEG: Time moves straight forward in a line. When you gave the ring back in the forest—we stepped out of time for a moment.

SUE: And it went on without us.

MEG: Thirty years have gone by. The adamite mines ran out.

SUE: Nobody goes up there any more.

HANNAH: Thirty years? But we left only yesterday.

MEG: Oh, no, dearie.

[TOOMEY *and* HANNAH *look all around in amazement.*]

HANNAH [*wonderingly*]: It must be true. Nothing else would explain it.

TOOMEY: Then—are we back in time again *now*?

MEG [*chuckling*]: Does it really matter?

FRED [*returning with tea tray, which he places on little table*]: Good thing you two have come back; we can do with some young faces about the place. Some people think it's almost *too* quiet now. [*He pours* MEG *a cup of tea.*]

[*"The Street Song" begins playing.* HANNAH *and* TOOMEY *smile at each other, walk hand in hand to centre, and begin to dance. Other* VILLAGERS *join them. The dance becomes more active. Tempo quickens. Drumming of hoofs is heard. Group assembles, looking towards side of stage as at start of Act One.*]

VILLAGERS: *The bulls! The bulls are coming! The bulls are coming back!*

[CURTAIN]

Street by Joan Aiken was produced by the Unicorn Theatre for Young People and was first performed on November 5, 1977, at the Arts Theatre, London, England.

Cast of Characters

Meg Mirkin	Gabrielle Hamilton
Hannibal Mirkin	Roland Oliver
Toomey Mirkin	Hugh Trethowan
Fred Steele	Ray Roberts
Lily Steele	Ursula Jones
Hannah Steele	Penny Casdagli
Sue Thatcher	Celia Hewitt
Jenny Thatcher	Christine Absalom
Bert, the hamburger man	Ian Ruskin
A truck driver	Steve Tindall
Villagers	Andrew Greenhalgh
	Henry Sharples

Director	Nicholas Barter
Designer	Russell Craig
Music Director	Ilona Sekacz
Lighting Designer	Angus Stewart
Music composed by	John Sebastian Brown

Songs

THE STREET SONG

If you want to keep your hands and arms,
And your legs and knees and feet,
Look to the right, look to the left,
Look to the right a-gain, look to the left a-gain
And then: don't cross the street!

CHORUS
Nev-er cross the street, Nev-er
cross the street. If you want to claim your
old-age pen-sion, Nev-er cross the street in Street.

If you want to keep a head that will think
And a heart with a regular beat,
Look to the right, look to the left, etc.

Repeat chorus

If life is your favourite habit,
And death is not your treat,
Look to the right, look to the left, etc.

Repeat chorus

If you want to live in a healthy spot
That's off the normal beat
Don't go to France, don't go to Spain
Don't go to Florida, don't go to Mexico—
But just: come down to Street!

CHORUS
Life is sweet in Street,
Life is sweet in Street!
Live to a hundred on your old-age pension,
Come along and live in Street.

THE HELICOPTER SONG

Here comes the heli-
Here comes the heli-
    copter bringing us our post.
A note for Mrs. Kelly,
A box for Mr. Shelley,

And a card for little Nelly
    from her cousins on the coast.
With *Guardian, Times* and Tele,
Comics, Penguins, Peli-
Cans—and parcel for mine host.

CHORUS: (as above)

TOOMEY AND HANNAH'S SONG

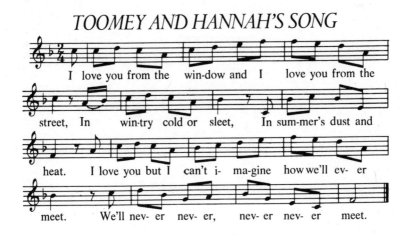

I love you from the win-dow and I love you from the street, In win-try cold or sleet, In sum-mer's dust and heat. I love you but I can't i- ma-gine how we'll ev- er meet. We'll nev- er nev- er, nev- er nev- er meet.

HANNAH: I love you through the window and I love you through the wall.
During all that may befall,
I'll love you best of all,
But oh, my love, I don't believe we'll ever meet at all.
I don't believe we'll ever meet at all!

BOTH: I love you more than sun or moon or cheese with apple tart.
I will give you all my heart
For I'm pierced by Cupid's dart,
But oh, my dearest angel, we are doomed to live apart.
My dearest, we are doomed to live apart.

HANNAH: I love you through the hours of dark, I love you through the day,
But attend to what I say:
There's danger in delay!
I think they'll even kill me if I don't do what they say.
They'll kill me if I don't do what they say!

TOOMEY: The best laid schemes of mice and men quite often gang a-gley,
So attend to what I say:
You'll *have* to disobey!
Why don't we get together and arrange to run away?
Why don't we just arrange to run away?

JENNY'S SONG

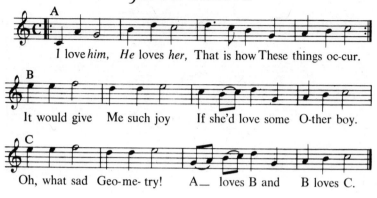

I love *him*, *He* loves *her*, That is how These things oc-cur.

It would give Me such joy If she'd love some O-ther boy.

Oh, what sad Geo-me-try! A— loves B and B loves C.

[*sung very softly and resignedly*]

A JENNY

Why does this
Have to be?
Why, oh why
Can't *he* love *me*?

B JENNY

Which might then
Leave him free
Just to take a
Look at *me*.

C JENNY

Such are Love's
Spiteful spells.
Why can't B love
Someone else?

But! [*spoken*]

A JENNY

He loves *her*.
She loves *him*.
So my outlook's
Rather grim.

A JENNY

I love *him*,
He loves *her*.
That's the way
These things occur.

B TOOMEY *and* HANNAH

I love *you*,
You love *me*.
Oh, how blessed by
Luck are we.

You love me,
I love you.
There is nothing
Else to do.

THE HAMBURGER SONG

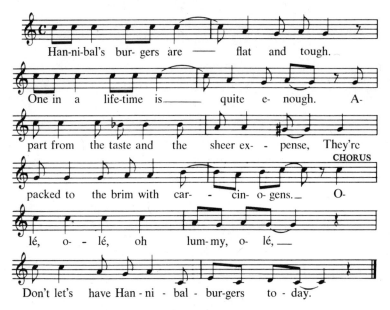

Han-ni-bal's bur- gers are ——— flat and tough.

One in a life-time is_____ quite e- nough. A-

part from the taste and the sheer ex- - pense, They're

packed to the brim with car- - cin- o- gens._ **CHORUS** O-

lé, o- - lé, oh lum-my, o- lé, ——

Don't let's have Han - ni - bal - bur-gers to - day.

Hannibalburgers are red as ruby.
Only a blind, besotted booby
Would ever suspend his disbelief
Enough to assume they were made of beef.

Repeat chorus

Swallow the bun at a single gulp.
It's made from coloured inflated pulp,
A mixture of softwood and Styrofoam.
Oh, what a feast for a gastronome!

Repeat chorus

Hannibalburgers are made from blubber,
Polythene bags, and cable rubber,
Insulation from telephone wires,
And miles of minced-up bicycle tyres.

Repeat chorus

VILLAGERS' LAMENT FOR JENNY

(Tune: "Poor Jenny Sits A-weeping")

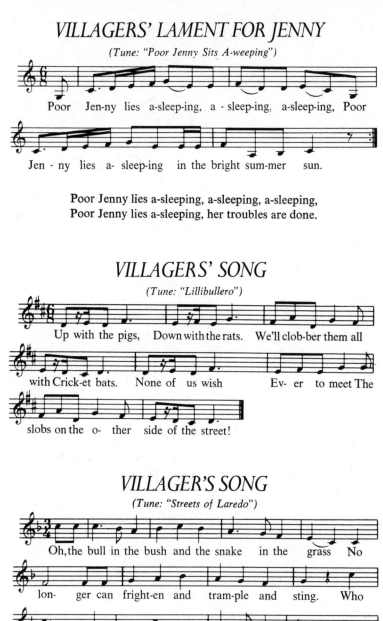

Poor Jen-ny lies a-sleep-ing, a - sleep-ing, a-sleep-ing, Poor

Jen - ny lies a- sleep-ing in the bright sum-mer sun.

Poor Jenny lies a-sleeping, a-sleeping, a-sleeping,
Poor Jenny lies a-sleeping, her troubles are done.

VILLAGERS' SONG

(Tune: "Lillibullero")

Up with the pigs, Down with the rats. We'll clob-ber them all

with Crick-et bats. None of us wish Ev- er to meet The

slobs on the o- ther side of the street!

VILLAGER'S SONG

(Tune: "Streets of Laredo")

Oh, the bull in the bush and the snake in the grass No

lon- ger can fright-en and tram-ple and sting. Who

cares for them now as the trucks thun-der past?__ Who

cares for the pow'r of an old mag- ic ring?

The snake in the grass and the bull in the bush
No longer can plague us with fear or with grief.
The serpent can't sting us, the bull cannot rush us,
The snake is a belt—and the bull is roast beef!

HANNIBAL'S SONG

(Tune: "My Bonnie Lies over the Ocean")

When I take out my chick in the chop-per,— The cher-ubs come
chirp-ing a - round— For an- y- thing's per-fect- ly prop-er—
When you're eight-y feet up from the ground.———

FOREST SONG

List-en to the for- est List- en to its
voi- ces List-en to the whis- per Of leaves and
stems and grass- es Green—breath-ing—
si- lent— calm Hold here—no thought of harm
Wise wood proud trees Love here—lives at ease.

Listen to the whisper
Listen: understand,
Nothing here can hurt you
The forest is your friend.

ABOUT THE AUTHOR

The daughter of the poet Conrad Aiken and the sister of two professional writers, Joan Aiken began writing at the age of five because, as she says, "Writing is just the family trade."

Joan Aiken has had published nearly thirty books for adults and children alike. *The Far Forests: Tales of Romance, Fantasy, and Suspense* and *The Skin Spinners,* a book of poems, were recently published by Viking. She lives in Sussex, England, and in New York City.